NEW DIRECTIONS
FOR TEACHING AND
LEARNING

Number 1 • 1980

NEW DIRECTIONS FOR TEACHING AND LEARNING

A Quarterly Sourcebook
Kenneth E. Eble and John Noonan, Editors-in-Chief

Number 1, 1980

Improving Teaching Styles

Kenneth E. Eble
Editor

Jossey-Bass Inc., Publishers
San Francisco • Washington • London

IMPROVING TEACHING STYLES
New Directions for Teaching and Learning
Number 1, 1980
        Kenneth E. Eble, Editor

New Directions for Teaching and Learning is published quarterly
by Jossey-Bass Inc., Publishers. Subscriptions are available
at the regular rate for institutions, libraries, and agencies
of $30 for one year. Individuals may subscribe at the special
professional rate of $18 for one year.

Correspondence:
Subscriptions, single-issue orders, change of address notices,
undelivered copies, and other correspondence should be sent to
New Directions Subscriptions, Jossey-Bass Inc., Publishers,
433 California Street, San Francisco, California 94104.
Editorial correspondence should be sent to the Editors-in-Chief,
Kenneth E. Eble or John Noonan, Department of English,
University of Utah, Salt Lake City, Utah 84112.

Library of Congress Catalogue Card Number LC 79-90236

Cover design by Willi Baum
Manufactured in the United States of America

Contents

Editor's Notes

Every teacher develops a particular way of going about the complex task of teaching. The way one introduces a topic, raises questions, makes assignments, talks to students after class—all these and hundreds of other particulars of behavior together make up a teacher's identification by colleagues and students. The more distinctive these characteristics are, the more they seem an integral part of who the person is and the more likely they are to be identified as his or her style.

This sourcebook attempts to probe some of the mysteries of style. A number of authors confront the matter of teaching style directly, attempt to define style, give examples of distinctive styles, and reflect on how style may be acquired and put to effective use. Other chapters examine more specifically teacher behaviors, particularly in terms of how behaviors may be shaped to best serve the ends of learning. The authors were chosen to represent a range of disciplines—from biochemistry and genetics to business management and philosophy—to reflect upon teaching style and its relation to learning, to synthesize research on specific aspects of teaching behavior, and to set forth practical experiences in working with faculty behaviors and developing teaching styles.

Joseph Axelrod's chapter follows one of the artist-teachers he profiled in *The University Teacher as Artist* (1973) into the late 1970s as he confronts the consequences of the counterrevolution that has turned back most of the reforms of the sixties. What Professor Abbot faces is the unease that seems to be pervasive among university professors at the end of this decade. The implications are as serious for students and administrators as for teachers and raise as many questions about the aims of higher education as about the way one goes about trying to further learning. The next chapter, by a philosophy professor at the University of Georgia, looks at developing teaching styles among graduate assistants; such teachers are crucial to the instructional programs of large universities yet are generally ill served as measured by what could be done to develop their skills as apprentice teachers. The third of this first group of personal experience chapters considers another sort of a teaching career. Edward Glassman, a tenured professor in a medical school, tells how he confronted his own needs and those of his students and radically revised his teaching strategies and style. Glassman's description of a teaching style which shifts attention away from the professor who lectures at students is in keeping with major developments of the past two decades.

Mary Lynn Crow brings together much of what has emerged from the study of group processes of learning. Teaching and learning are described as interactive processes, and the effective teacher is one who has a command of the various ways of facilitating interaction.

The focus of the last three chapters is upon ways of working with faculty behaviors within college and university structures. Bette and Glenn Erickson draw upon their experiences in the instructional development program at the University of Rhode Island, with an emphasis on working with faculty members to assist them in changing their teaching behaviors. Seeing ourselves as others see us is a necessary part of the ability to change, and of the growth in personality and character which underlies the development of an effective teaching style. Technology has given us the means of seeing our behaviors, and Richard and Margaret Ishler cover the extensive research that has been done in the use of observation techniques and self-scrutiny through microteaching. The last chapter, by Peter Seldin, argues that more attention needs to be given to shaping behavior before the fact. Instead of leaving the acquisition of teaching behaviors to the general influences of the institutional press and specific requirements of the reward system, Seldin advocates growth contracts that set forth goals in advance and assist teachers in achieving such goals.

The complexities of the impact of teachers on students—or teaching's actual relationship with learning—are probably as great as those of the human mind. Trying to expand our knowledge of what John Granrose calls "the lesser and greater mysteries" of teaching is an obligation of formal research, institutional study and practice, and individual effort. These chapters, it is hoped, will help to provide formal documentation on teaching as well as practical assistance to individual readers.

Kenneth E. Eble
Guest Editor

Reference

Axelrod, J. *The University Teacher as Artist.* San Francisco: Jossey-Bass, 1973.

Kenneth E. Eble is professor of English and university professor 1976–1977 at the University of Utah.

Style, this chapter argues, is as important as character for the aspiring teacher. Customary academic behaviors may get in the way of developing both.

Teaching Styles and Faculty Behaviors

Kenneth E. Eble

Style in university teaching, like much else that pertains to teaching excellence, has been too little respected by teachers themselves. It has been confused with affectation, denigrated as a kind of posturing to mask a lack of substance, or tolerated as a natural manifestation of personal eccentricities. Seldom has it been recognized in the sense set forth by Buffon: "Le style est l'homme meme" (Style is the man himself). We speak of "teaching styles" but seldom mean more than whether one customarily lectures or leads discussions, or whether a teacher is rigid and demanding or spontaneous and encouraging. When style is conspicuous in a teacher, it is likely to be viewed pejoratively. The person is a showman, a popularizer, a crowd pleaser.

But, rightly viewed, style in teaching as in playing shortstop well or in conducting a criminal prosecution is not merely something put on for the occasion. As F. L. Lucas (1962) has said of style in writing, it is not "elegant mannerism," but "a means by which one personality moves others." In a different context (the style of administrators), D. McGregor (1967) says that a manager's style emerges "as a result of his lifetime of coping with reality" and is deeply rooted in "his fundamental beliefs, his values, his perception of himself, and his lifetime of experience."

To me, style as applied to teaching is not merely a high fashion concept, and research into the relationship between teaching styles and their impact on students gives some support to my contention. Both Wilson (Wilson, and others, 1975) and Yamamoto and Dizney (1966) have tried to ascertain relationships between teaching styles and student preferences which may, in turn, have an effect upon student achievements. From related studies, Tennyson, Boutwell, and Frey (1978) conclude that college students have "an overwhelming preference for a professor who sees himself, and is seen, as a teacher rather than researcher, administrator, or socialite" (Tennyson, Boutwell, and Frey, 1978, p. 196).

All teachers should recognize that a good style is essential to their rising above the veriest of mediocrities, that its acquisition is a whole and lifetime process, and that, though style may manifest itself in skills and techniques, the development of style involves much more than these. Nor should teachers be deterred from seeking an effective style by the fear or futility of arriving at *one* effective style. Edward Sheffield's book *Teaching in the Universities: No One Way* (1974) testifies to the varieties of highly effective teaching styles. Much of the faculty development movement concentrates on the acquiring of skills and techniques as a means of improving teaching. It is by now demonstrably true that university teachers can be developed in rather simple ways, such as adding to or updating their grasp of subject matter, improving their organization of materials, adding to their knowledge and use of technical adjuncts to teaching, and improving such specific skills as those of lecturing, discussing, testing, and grading.

What interests me here is stimulating further interest in the development of style as a fundamental and more complex aspect of a university teacher's preparation. Let me turn back to Lucas and his assertion that literary style is simply a means by which one personality moves another. As simple as that sounds, and as applicable as it is to teaching, acceptance of a large role for personality in teaching comes hard for a university faculty. I do not know just why this is so. Certainly teaching at the university level excites sufficient personal vanities to suggest that a concern for personality is not altogether absent. And only a very foolish person would deny that we are all powerfully influenced by the personalities of those we listen to and learn from. Perhaps we shy away from personality in teaching because, up until very recently, the scientific outlook which dominates higher education still touted impersonal, objective truth. (It is not that we have abandoned that belief but that we are coming to see the personal character of much that passes for objective truth and we are less certain of the possibility of arriving at that objective truth.) Or it may be that the detached, necessarily isolated (at times) behavior characteristic of the scholar attracts to university faculties numbers of those who are, in both good and bad senses, relatively devoid of personality. A philosopher/mathematician of my acquaintance has been bold enough to say that mathematics attracts the self-contained and inner-directed and that mathematicians, as a group, tend to possess traits that as a rule do not characterize effective classroom instruction. "We convince," Whitman said, "by our presence." Given the conventions and structures and physical arrangements that shape university teaching, the teacher's personality is an important fact, undeniable in any common-sense notion of teaching, and worthy of more consideration than it is commonly given.

Perhaps faculty members troubled about the place of personality in a teacher's style would be less troubled — or troubled in a different way — if we shifted the emphasis to character. "The first thing in style," so Lucas (1962, p. 52) says, "is character." The same might be said, should be said, of style in teaching. There is a long-established linkage between character and style from Socrates to Aristotle to Buffon and Gibbon and beyond. In Gibbon's phrasing, "Style is the image of character." To me, it follows that the proper preparation for a teacher is an education in self close to the old-fashioned notion that education aims importantly at developing character. Without character, a teacher is more ill equipped than if he or she had not mastered the table of elements, Shakespeare's tragedies, or harmony and counterpoint.

Very little of this kind of thinking affects the graduate school, which does most to shape a university professor's immediate stance toward teaching. No self-respecting graduate school has shown the least interest in character. And though present faculty development movements and teaching improvement efforts aim at the acquisition of skills and techniques, such skills and techniques will not in themselves result in an admirable style.

What might be done, then, to foster the development of style, not as a mere reflection of a teacher's characteristic practices or the sum of a teacher's mastery of techniques, but as that which underlies all effective practices? First of all, I think, must be a continuing attempt by all those seriously interested in teaching and those whose speaking and writing and administering and presence affects others to get style recognized for what it is and to encourage its development. Young teachers must not be allowed to take on the various mucker poses that can come out of the graduate school: that of abusing the authority that a little learning seems to confer, of fastening their specialized pedantries upon liberal education, of catering to the paper reading, publishing, and proposal writing that builds academic reputations. Nor must exceptional teachers who do link style and character and mastery of subject matters be let off by their own humility before the mysteries of great teaching. Mystery does not necessarily suffer from being thoughtfully pondered and expounded.

Similarly, research into teaching styles must not let itself be severed from dimensions of style not easily observed or explained. Indeed, almost all research into teaching suffers by comparison with the vibrancy of the act itself, and suffers badly from isolating in order to analyze, from systematizing in order to simplify, from embracing terminology, charts, print-outs — in order to what? Deceive ourselves and the public and win foundation grants?

Finally, faculty development movements need to see the development of teaching competence in relation to personality and character as well as to techniques and skills. Three examples of what I mean will suffice. One recognizable model of working with faculty as teachers is the clinical one. I do not much like the term "clinical" and I am wary of many "clinicians," but I am also impressed with some sensitive work going on. Bette and Glenn Erickson at the University of Rhode Island work chiefly with techniques and strategies, but they recognize the uniqueness of a professor's teaching style, and the need to recognize this individuality in working to improve effectiveness. What the Ericksons do can fairly be inferred from the faculty members with whom they have consulted who were asked to identify the most important features of the process. The most frequent comments were "the opportunity to talk with someone about my teaching," "the systematic nature of the analysis and improvement procedures," and "the personal interest and support provided by the instructional development consultant" (Erickson and Erickson, n.d.). A second example is Kiyo Morimoto's use of audio and video tape at Harvard. Seeing ourselves somewhat as others see us and criticizing with our colleagues aspects of teaching performance can have a marked impact on developing an effective style. A number of films sensitively isolate critical moments in teaching likely to elicit from viewers thoughts not only about strategies but about teaching style itself. Students furnish still another source of enlarging faculty member's perceptions of themselves. The work of John Noonan at Virginia Commonwealth and of Robert Wilson at Berkeley are good examples of using students in this way.

If, as I have argued, teaching style is not given sufficient attention, customary faculty behaviors are all too palpable in their impact upon teaching. To draw upon the analogy with writing once again, I can argue that across a university, faculty perform about as well or as badly as teachers as they do as writers. Most — not all — faculty members can write a reasonably serviceable prose adequate to communication within the peculiarities of their disciplines. Not one in ten of that number has any distinctive style even as measured against what passes for writing well in the discipline. Not one in 50 or 500 has a distinguished writing style as measured against effective prose over its long history as a carrier of thought and an inciter of emotion. The proportions are probably not far different as regards teachers. Most college faculty members have enough of character and personality, skills and techniques, to teach at a level their departments and disciplines find tolerable. A greatly reduced number can be singled out as possessing a distinguished style as measured by their colleagues. And fewer still will have a style that measures up against more demanding comparisons.

Why this is so is lodged, I think, in faculty behaviors more easily acquired than style and as persistent as the bad habits of our youth. One such behavior is to gravitate to the easiest teaching load possible. Another is to move toward the best students as measured by some narrow standard compatible with a professor's reduction of life to an approximation of his own world. Another is to be guided in techniques and practices by the routes of least resistance: to favor the lecture, to shun innovations and adjuncts to instruction, to reduce teaching chiefly to class preparation and delivery on as few hours a week as possible and at the most convenient times. Too few see teaching as a kind of day and night occupation in which one is always on call. Another set of faculty behaviors are those which shape the university in ways which can reduce teaching to its most convenient dimensions: to adopt and uphold selective admissions policies, to maintain an inflexible grading system, to contrive requirements and prerequisites to keep people out or flunk them out, to limit withdrawals and exceptions to policies, to cling to calendars favorable to the professor's work, and to maintain a curriculum chiefly reflective of faculty specializations and self-interest.

I do not cite these behaviors as manifested by all faculty every place and at all times. Those with a keen memory of the late 1960s in the United States may dispute most of these claims. I would respond merely by saying the 1960s are over, the behaviors I am talking about are back in force, and they probably never would have been dislodged except by the presence of great numbers of students forcing faculties to face chronic complaints. In short, I do not think "character" is in excess supply among faculty members, and the development of a truly admirable teaching style involves the development of character which, in turn, often involves giving up comfortable behaviors. Beyond that, developing an exemplary teaching style is to be achieved by painstaking and loving and artful attention to the particulars of what one does—both as a person and teacher. That is not meant to endorse a constant watching of oneself in classroom or out, but neither does it endorse willful or witless ignoring of what we are and what we do as teachers and persons. An admirable style will not come early—for a teacher it should be expected to emerge in some fullness only with some fullness of years. Given the right grounding in character, the willingness to grant personality its importance, and the favorable climate in which to develop, one may arrive at an admirable style by the route of inatten-

6

tion to style itself. But, given shallow roots in character, an ill adjustment with self, and little of nurture in the climate, the development of even an effective style may need attention from within as well as wise aid from without. Established with some firmness, then, style does indeed show forth without the solicitude that seems to compromise it — as unnatural as it is, it will appear all the more natural, all the more pleasing.

References

Lucas, F. L. *Style.* New York: Collier Books, 1962.

McGregor, D. *The Professional Manager.* New York: McGraw-Hill, 1967.

Sheffield, E. *Teaching in the Universities: No One Way.* Montreal: McGill-Queens University Press, 1974.

Tennyson, R. D., Boutwell, R. C., and Frey, S. "Student Preferences for Faculty Teaching Styles." *Improving College and University Teaching,* 1978, *26* (3), 194–197.

Wilson, R. C., and others. *College Professors and Their Impact on Students.* New York: Wiley, 1975.

Yamamoto, K., and Dizney, H. F. "Eight Professors: A Study on College Students' Preferences Among Their Teachers." *Journal of Educational Psychology,* 1966, *57,* 146–150.

Kenneth E. Eble is professor of English and university professor 1976–77 at the University of Utah. His writings on higher education began with The Profane Comedy: American Higher Education in the Sixties *for Macmillan in 1962 and have continued in books, newspaper columns, and magazine and journal articles. His last two books for Jossey-Bass were* The Art of Administration *(1978) and* The Craft of Teaching *(1976).*

This profile of a college professor's career, 1959–1984, focuses on changes in teaching style which in turn reflect teaching philosophy, student characteristics, and institutional shifts.

From Counterculture to Counterrevolution: A Teaching Career

Joseph Axelrod

When the year 1984 arrives, Professor Stephen Abbot will have completed his twenty-fifth year of college teaching. When he began his teaching career in 1959, a new era in American higher education had also just begun, and it was clear by the mid 1960s that an academic revolution was in the making. Abbot took part in that revolution, and his teaching style changed radically. Then, in the mid 1970s, the revolution was suddenly over and during the next few years Abbot slowly realized that the gains of that revolution had all but disappeared. Around 1979, he came to the conviction that there had been a counterrevolution in teaching and learning at American universities, and it had taken place so quietly he had not even been aware of it.

Overview: 1959–1979

When Stephen Abbot's teaching career began in 1959, Sputnik was still fresh in everyone's mind. The American government, responding quickly to this momentous Russian advance in the cold war, had rallied its resources to the cause of "national defense." Counted among the nation's resources were its colleges and universities, and by the fall of 1959, funds authorized by the National Defense Education Act of 1958 were being channeled to many campuses all across the country.

The spread and growth of a new "type" of institution of higher education—what Kerr (1963) called the Federal Grant University—was only one of a dozen or more signs that pointed to the inauguration of a new era. Another was the growing centralization of higher education. When Abbot moved to the San Francisco Bay Area to assume his new teaching post, he discovered that higher education in California was an expanding universe. To his surprise, however, it was a rather tightly controlled universe, thanks to a new state master plan for higher education that had been drawn up in the late 1950s and enacted into law in 1960. Within a few years, master plans for higher education were developed in a half-dozen other states as well.

Another sign of the new era was the growing unrest among students and faculty members, many of whom began to display their dissatisfaction openly in the late 1950s. Responsible critiques of higher education at all levels began to appear, among them those of Carmichael (1961) on graduate education, McGrath (1959) on liberal education, Medsker (1960) on junior colleges, and Henderson (1960) on higher education policies and practices. Nevitt Sanford (1962) concluded that "American colleges are failing rather badly. They fail to achieve their own stated purposes; and they fail by other reasonable standards of accomplishment" (p. 2).

College professors called the decade of the 1950s apathetic. Students refused to become involved with the subject matter of their college studies or the problems with which society was then confronted. David Riesman described the students of that period as "a generation of gamesmen." But toward the end of the 1950s, apathy gave way to activism. The student voice became an important factor in determining the direction of educational reform on campus and in influencing political decisions in the country at large. An early event in the student movement was a demonstration against the House Un-American Activities Committee, which was conducting hearings at the San Francisco City Hall. The demonstration ended when hundreds of students from Stanford, Berkeley, and San Francisco State were washed down the steps of City Hall by policemen wielding fire hoses. Equally significant—but scarcely noticed at the time by the general public—was a statement of "Student Concerns" that was presented to the administration at Berkeley in 1958. These concerns, quoted in Axelrod and others, *Search for Relevance* (1969), were both curricular and educational as well as political, and anticipated to a high degree student demands of 1964.

Abbot had not yet arrived in California when these expressions of dissatisfaction were taking place. He was aware of the events and regarded them with considerable interest, but he did not yet grasp their significance in the history of American higher education. During his years as a graduate student in the field of English, Abbot had been thoroughly "socialized," and he had accepted the public image that the universities themselves had projected. Even during his first years as a college teacher, he did not feel that anything could seriously be wrong with higher education in this country. But the cry of "Relevance!" was already in the air, and by the early 1960s, after his arrival in California, Abbot began to feel the pressures for change and to recognize that the patterns of teaching and learning on American campuses could not remain what they had been.

Abbot's own classroom practices did not undergo very much change until about 1964. Until that time, his teaching style was modeled largely on the behavior of his own college teachers of literature; his image of himself strongly resembled his memory of them. His job as a teacher of literature, he was convinced, was to teach *literature*. He knew, of course, that he was teaching students, but the focus of his attention was placed on the subject matter of his courses. As a consequence, there was an impersonal atmosphere in his classrooms. He liked his students well enough, but he was not very much interested in them as individuals — in an important sense he did not "care" about them as people — and he did not expect them, for their part, to be interested in him as a person.

That first stage in Abbot's development as a teacher lasted for about five years. Then, sometime around 1964, Abbot's teaching style changed. His new attitude toward teaching had been gradually developing, he realized, and it was brought sharply into focus by the campus activity that surrounded the Free Speech Movement at Berkeley. His job, he now felt, was to teach *students*. He went on teaching them literature, of course, but his central concern was now the individual student, not the subject matter. He noted with satisfaction that his students responded enthusiastically to this shift in emphasis, and the atmosphere in his classrooms noticeably warmed.

The change from a teaching style focused on subject matter to a student-centered teaching style was not as great as the labels might suggest, however. In this second stage in Abbot's development, he focused his attention on the student — but not on the *whole* student. The learning mode fostered by Abbot was fairly narrow in range. Analytic and rational, it emphasized the development of linguistic and linear modes of perception. In short, Abbot was training the intellects of his students. He had always recognized the presence — and even the power — of nonanalytic modes of consciousness in the learning process, but he did not believe it was his job to seek to develop them in a student. Indeed, he was not even persuaded that nonanalytic modes of consciousness could be learned in a university class or that a professor of literature should attempt to teach them.

After 1964, Abbot was for some years satisfied with his new

approach. But his teaching style was not permanently fixed — it was, in fact, gradually developing. Toward the end of the 1960s, Abbot became aware that he had in many ways again altered his view, and by the spring of 1970, when the invasion of Cambodia and the tragic events at Kent State and Jackson State took place, he realized that his philosophy of teaching had undergone a reversal. He now believed that teachers, if they hoped to be effective in any profound way, had to look upon a student as a whole person, not merely as a "mind" to be trained.

This new conception influenced Abbot's teaching style in fundamental ways. He was still teaching students, and he was still teaching them literature, but his teaching was now based on an entirely different notion of what students are. In this third stage in Abbot's development, beginning about 1970, he entered a different relationship with his students. The atmosphere in his classrooms became intensely personalized. He became a learner along with his students. He was a more experienced learner, to be sure, but the difference was one of degree and not of kind. He wanted students to see him as a pursuer of knowledge rather than a master of it. And, above all, they were to see him as their friend as well as their critic.

While this third stage of development lasted, Abbot was very happy in his work. But around 1975, he began to feel that something was not quite right. For one thing, the curricular reforms of the 1960s that he had so vigorously supported were beginning to crumble, not only on his own campus but all over the country. Moreover, a new kind of student was beginning to appear in the universities, and this new student, it was evident, felt no responsibility and no sense of commitment to academic pursuits or to society. Abbot and his colleagues began to describe them as the "Me Generation" of students.

Once again, but more slowly this time, Abbot's teaching style underwent a change. The shift was inevitable because a new kind of relationship was required for dealing with this new kind of student. It was true, of course, that in each of his classes, Abbot found a few students who displayed a commitment to their studies, and he continued to care about them personally. But for most of his students he no longer had any personal feeling. They began, in fact, to lose their individual identity. He could no longer fix his attention on them while he was teaching. More and more, his attention reverted to his own concerns as a scholar, and these concerns now became the focal point of his teaching.

His class sessions were now devoted mainly to his own insights, his own ideas, his own modes of perception, his own methods of solving problems in the field of literary studies. He prepared for his classes as conscientiously as ever, and he made his class presentations as attractive as possible. His classes were rarely dull, and they were often exciting. But the atmosphere was largely depersonalized. The students could learn or not—according to their own desires. Except for the handful of committed students, Abbot no longer cared much about them as individuals. In the twenty years that had elapsed since 1959, he had come full circle.

During this fourth stage in his development as a teacher, Abbot became convinced that a counterrevolution had taken place. The reforms in teaching and learning that had taken place in the 1960s had not lasted. They had disappeared *very* quickly, and Abbot felt that he had somehow been tricked into joining the counterrevolutionaries— why and how he did not know. The counterrevolution had already succeeded before he realized what was happening.

We need now to take a closer look at the details of Abbot's teaching career if we wish to detect the sources of the counterrevolution—as they affected Abbot's classroom behavior—and trace their movement. If the reader is to follow our probe with ease, however, we must first present the theoretical framework that provides the crucial terms of our analysis.

Theoretical Framework

Professor Abbot first became the subject of a case study in college teaching some ten years ago when the present writer was directing an investigation of teaching styles under the auspices of the Center for Research and Development in Higher Education at the University of California, Berkeley (Axelrod, 1973). At that time, a theoretical framework was developed within which an analysis of teaching styles could be made. This framework postulates that the teaching-learning process is a dynamic relationship in which three elements are in constant interaction: the individual (or individuals) assuming the teacher roles, the individual (or individuals) playing learner roles, and the subject matters that are being taught or learned. For the purposes of the framework, the term *subject matter* includes not only facts and principles which are committed to memory but everything capable of being taught and learned: skills and competencies, abilities, attitudes and habits, concepts and theories, modes of "processing data," and the like

If a professor were to describe the dynamic relationship which is the teaching-learning process as he or she would *wish* it to be, that statement would constitute a description of the professor's "mode" of teaching. (As the phrase *teaching style* is used here, it is synonymous with *teaching mode.*) In the framework of this theory, then, a professor's teaching mode is a mental prototype. It is, in the most important sense, an intention, a vision of how a class session (or series of class sessions) *ought* to go.

Teaching modes may be characterized as "appropriate" or

"inappropriate" for certain educational ends, but no particular teaching mode, according to this theory, can be characterized as "excellent" or "poor." Since the teaching mode is a mental prototype, only its realization in the hands of a particular professor can be judged to be excellent or poor. Moreover, such a judgment is unusually complex; it cannot be made by an observer who does not understand the professor's intention, the vision of the class that exists in the professor's mind. The observer receives the clearest, most concrete view of the professor's teaching style, of course, when the discrepancy between the mental prototype and the external behaviors is minimal—that is, when the professor's intention is most fully realized.

The theory postulates four mental prototypes or teaching modes. They can be differentiated by examining the relationship among the three elements in the teaching-learning process: the teacher, the student, and the subject matter. In that relationship, as it comes into existence during any teaching-learning session, one of these three elements is dominant and the other two elements must accommodate themselves to its demands and its requirements.

When the dynamic relationship centers dominantly on *subject matter,* the other two elements undergo "adjustment." For example, in cases where the content of a course has been rigidly set, the subject matter must be covered even if the professor or the learners have special requirements that may be antagonistic to the subject matter coverage. Professors ordinarily have the power to reshape the subject matter, but if they follow this teaching mode, they view with alarm any suggestion that the content of the course should be changed in order to facilitate the teaching-learning process. They fear, for example, that their colleagues will accuse them of lowering academic standards. To change the subject matter in any basic way in order to accommodate the special needs of a group of students, the argument goes, would be detrimental to the university and, in the long run, to the students themselves.

Professors whose courses focus on the *student* rather than on subject matter voice a different kind of concern. They believe that the teaching-learning process will not be effective if conditions require the student to be vastly reshaped before the process can begin. After all, the argument of these professors asserts, all aspects of the college enterprise—classes and courses, professors and deans and business officers, stadiums and dormitories—exist to meet the needs of the students as growing human beings.

When the teaching model focuses on the *professor,* it is characterized by the professor's attitude toward his or her own role. Whether the professor plays the role of shaman, priest, or mystic healer, the role of model learner, scholar-specialist, or debonair intellectual, in this teaching mode it is always the teacher who is at the center of the process, and the other two elements in the interaction are obliged to accommodate themselves to the requirements of that relationship.

In each of these three models, the *purpose* of the teaching-learning interaction is conceived differently. Those professors who focus on subject matter organize their teaching around one unambiguous goal: to help the student *master* selected principles, concepts, analytic tools, theories, applications, relevant facts, and the like. The class session is characterized by two main features: an emphasis on cognitive knowledge that is considered "standard" in the field, and the systematic coverage of a definite segment of that knowledge.

Professors who focus on themselves — on their own methods and ideas — organize class sessions around a different goal: to help the student learn to approach problems in the field as they themselves approach them. Like their colleagues who focus on subject matter, they concentrate on transmitting segments of knowledge that are considered "standard" in the field. But unlike those colleagues, they use the force of their own personalities and their own unique points of view to give shape to that knowledge. As a result, their students are more likely to acquire attitudes and viewpoints that the professors transmit on the affective level. Usually in this model, however, knowledge in the affective domain is secondary to knowledge in the cognitive domain.

For those professors who focus on the student, a distinction must be made between two different teaching models. There are professors who emphasize the development of the student but limit the scope of their endeavor to what many psychologists and neurophysiologists have in recent years identified as "left-hemisphere" brain activity — that is, linear, rational, verbal thinking. These professors insist that their students use reason and language as their major analytic tools and the problem-solving process as the major means of investigating the subject matter.

The other type of student-centered professor takes a holistic approach, hoping to educate *both* hemispheres of the brain. Professors who follow this teaching style emphasize the personal development of the whole student, organizing class sessions around the desire to help students develop as individuals along all dimensions. The aim is to improve not only the students' analytic skills but also their ability to use their intuitive nonverbal powers, and to react to themselves and the world in a variety of nonlinear, nonrational modes as well as in the step-by-step linear mode.

Stephen Abbot's Development

From 1959 to 1979, Stephen Abbot searched for the teaching style that would best fit his own and his students' needs. In this search, he moved through four stages, and those four stages represent the four models that have just been described: the subject matter-centered model, the two student-centered models, and the instructor-centered model.

Stage I: 1959–1964. When Abbot began his career as a teacher, he had a clear picture of his goals and the teaching style that would best achieve those goals. His focus was on the subject matter—in fact, a question about whether any other focus was possible never occurred to him. As a teacher of literature, his goal was simple and direct. He tried to transmit to his students some insights into the meanings of selected literary works and into the place of those works and their authors in the Western literary tradition.

Although Abbot lectured occasionally during those early years, he believed that students learn better when they are active in the class. Thus, though he did lecture, discussion was an important aspect of his style. As a discussion leader, Abbot clearly understood what duties he had to perform. It was his job, for example, to keep the discussion moving without long and embarrassing pauses. More important, he was the one to decide when to introduce each new topic, to make statements summarizing the topics already discussed, and to avoid tangential issues so that the discussion could remain controlled. Abbot never for a moment considered that the class as a whole, or any students in it, might wish—or should be asked—to undertake any of the responsibilities he had assigned to himself. He was the teacher, and only he had the right to play the teacher role.

Although Abbot liked his students and cared about some of them deeply, the general atmosphere in his classrooms was impersonal. Even in those years, many professors were beginning to use first names when addressing students, especially in small group discussion classes, but Abbot used only last names. And of course no student could, at that time, have called him "Steve."

Stage II: 1964–1970. During the mid 1960s, Abbot, like his colleagues, began to respond to insistent student pressures. Gradually he became committed to the principle that his job was not to teach courses but to train young minds. His style shifted to a student-centered mode. In his beginning courses in literature, his new attitude translated itself into a complex and rigorous method of interpreting literary texts. His students were expected to arrive at an interpretation of a work and were called upon to demonstrate to their classmates how this interpretation fit or illuminated various parts and details of the work. Analysis was the dominant mode of communication in his classes. An intuition about the meaning of a work was not rejected out of hand, but Abbot insisted that it had to be tested. He taught students how to look for evidence, how to read data, how to set one's starting points, and how to become aware of the terms of one's own (or a critic's) dialectic.

The emphasis of Abbot's teaching during those years was placed strongly on student development, but he limited his interest mainly to intellectual development. Although he prided himself on the rigor of his teaching methods, he pointed out to his subject matter-oriented colleagues that he was concerned with the growth of his students' intellectual abilities and not with their acquisition of informational knowledge. He did not share his colleagues' concerns about covering the "standard" knowledge of the field and about requiring students to learn textbook definitions of such terms as "Romanticism," "Realism," or "Transcendentalism." His objective, he explained, was to teach students to read literary works with sensitivity, and he hoped that his students, after they had left their courses with him, would be able — and would *want* — to pursue literary experiences with ease and enjoyment.

Stage III: 1970–1974. It was the events of the spring of 1970 — the Cambodian invasion, the killings at Kent State and Jackson State — that moved Abbot to a third stage in his search for a teaching style. During those months, Abbot moved away from the highly logical, rational framework of aesthetics and pedagogics that had characterized the mid 1960s stage of his development, and he emerged from the crisis of the spring of 1970 with new attitudes toward both his students and his educational goals.

Abbot now believed that his emphasis on intellectual development and rational activity had been based on a false principle: he realized that intellectual development cannot be split from other aspects of the human personality. And he concluded that an education that encourages fragmentation — such as a curriculum that focuses exclusively on the training of the intellect — must be regarded as having failed.

This concept, translated into classroom practice, led to a whole new ethos in Abbot's classes. The atmosphere was now intensely personal. "Caring" became a central responsibility for every member of the teaching-learning group, and "All are responsible for all" (*The Brothers Karamazov* was a key work in his classes during those years) became a kind of class motto. Steve, as his students came to call him, was not only their teacher and severest critic; he was also, and above all, their friend. Many of his students of those years are still his personal friends, even though they have long since given up their affiliation with the collegiate world.

The key to understanding Abbot's teaching style during this period lies in the phrase "student involvement." Abbot was concerned that his students involve themselves in their schoolwork in an intense way, and he believed that this involvement could not come about unless their school activities became inextricably bound up with their daily lives. To that end he adopted as a strategy a requirement that students discuss the novels and plays that they were reading for his course with their friends and parents — especially with their parents.

Abbot also encouraged his young students to try out adult roles in situations where they felt somewhat unsure, for he understood their uncertainty, expecially during their early college years, as they moved from adolescence to adulthood. This uncertainty, he noticed, was particularly prevalent among students who came from upwardly mobile families who were in the lower half of the socioeconomic spectrum. The son in such a family, for instance, ordinarily has little to say to his mother. When he does talk with her, he usually speaks of some family matter, and his relationship to her thus remains a mother-child relationship. But if the class is reading Isherwood's *Berlin Stories,* and if the student can be persuaded to talk to his mother about Sally Bowles' love affairs, then the likelihood is that the son will speak to his mother as an adult.

The main purpose of all this was that Abbot wanted literature to serve his students in their growth as *people* and to confirm them in their status as adults. He wanted literature to become a natural part of their lives — he did not want it to remain something that they did for school and would want to stop doing as soon as they stopped going to school. But there was also another purpose. When students took the initiative and started a discussion at home about a novel they were reading for Abbot's class, something subtle happened: they were, so to speak, making a public statement about their commitment to literature.

During Stage III of his development as a teacher, Abbot thus perfected a series of techniques — through his choice of reading and writing assignments, nontraditional term projects, new formats for examinations, and workshop-type class discussions — that helped him achieve success in his attempts to work with students as people.

Stage IV: 1974–1979. Sometime during 1974–1975, Abbot felt that a change was taking place in his classes, but he could not at first identify it. Except among a small group of especially conscientious students in each of his classes, a spirit of impersonality seemed to have taken over. It was a withdrawal of some kind, almost a fear on the part of the students, of becoming involved with the subject matter of the course or with the teacher.

Abbot discovered, moreover, that the approach to educational problems, especially curricular problems, exhibited by the administrative officers on his campus (and by many of his colleagues) was dominated by an emphasis on "career education" that very much resembled the curricular priorities of the 1950s when Abbot himself had been a graduate student and a teaching assistant in freshman courses. At the same time, "general education" became a stylish byword once again. With the upsurge of careerist goals, general education requirements which had been largely abolished during the 1960s were once more being widely discussed. When the "old" requirements were reinstituted at Harvard and Berkeley, they were acclaimed by Abbot's colleagues, and it was only a matter of time before they were reinstituted on Abbot's own campus as well.

In Abbot's view, most of these reforms seemed pointless — a return to the rather simple-minded degree patterns that were so common in the years following World War II. Since they had proved to be inadequate then, how could anyone imagine that they would be useful for the 1970s and beyond? Moreover, such reforms seemed to be motivated by or compromised by faculty self-interest, the need to maintain enrollments, or the need to get back to traditional, safer ways of teaching and pursuing scholarship.

Everywhere Abbot turned, he felt the same pressures arising from all quarters — government agencies, accrediting associations, disciplinary societies, higher education organizations, and the administrators and faculty members on his own campus. Worst of all, this regression (for this was what Abbot believed it to be) seemed to please the majority of the students as well. The students, it appeared, wanted to be given little responsibility for undertaking their own education. In fact, they were not really interested in education at all. On Abbot's campus the dormitories, which had remained partially empty during most of the 1960s, were now once again full to bursting, and their occupants were noisy, high-spirited, and fun-loving. Sororities and fraternities were active again, too, and they thrived on carnival-like atmospheres.

Abbot had difficulty accepting this turn of events. He had once viewed his campus as a community of scholars who loved learning, as a community of concerned individuals who cared about one another. But with each passing year, that image faded further and further away.

The new campus ethos had an enormous impact on Abbot. He found himself resisting the certain signs of a reactionary counterrevolution, yet he was unsure of the revolutionary stance he had once accepted. He found himself forced to adopt classroom behaviors that were far removed from his teaching style of the late 1960s and early 1970s. Ironically, he felt that his relationship to his students now bore a marked resemblance to the relationship his professors had had with him when he was a graduate student. He observed himself returning to the methods and attitudes that had characterized his early years as a teacher, and he once more became an authority figure who told his students what was important and what they must learn.

Reluctantly and yet conscientiously responding to internal as well as external pressures, Abbot found himself arriving at a fourth stage in his changing teaching style. Once again, his emphasis was on subject matter, not greatly concerned with students except as they were obviously the objects of instruction, not much concerned with wholeness, either of the student's development or of his own educational aims. In his present stage, the focus was on himself. His goal now was to provide students with a model of a professionally educated person, and he used his class time to demonstrate what such a person does with the materials of literature. The goal for his students was different too: they were not expected merely to master the subject matter (as in Stage I), but to demonstrate in their papers and on examinations that they could imitate his particular way of conceiving problems, defining their crucial terms, formulating them in scope, handling pertinent data, and working toward solutions.

During the years of Stage IV, Abbot could not carry on anything resembling (except in the most superficial aspects) the kind of discussion sessions that had characterized his classes during Stages II and III of his development. That kind of discussion session simply would not work with a group of students who were predominantly passive. His class meetings were now generally divided into two parts: lectures, followed by question-and-answer periods. While most of his students still remained passive, accepting what he offered them but not becoming deeply involved in his world, there formed in each class a small group of devoted and/or ambitious students who came to play a central role in the question-and-answer periods after the lectures. Usually, they would challenge Abbot's point of view, pointing out what they thought were inconsistencies in his lecture or raising questions about ideas presented by other literary historians and critics. Occasionally a student would present an alternative interpretation to Abbot's own. Abbot obviously enjoyed these challenges and encouraged them, and by employing a bit of showmanship that he made little effort to hide, he almost always emerged victorious. But he was aware that no one ever objected to the fact that he took advantage of his position at the podium. Students expected that as an authority figure, he would have — and deserved to have — the last word.

Abbot responded warmly to the students who gave evidence of involvement in his courses. Most of the students, however, gave no such evidence, although some of them pretended interest, and he was not especially interested in them. And even when he had good rapport with certain students, he found that their ideas, per se, had little importance for him. Where he used ideas expressed by his students, it was for the sake of highlighting his own ideas. All of his conversations with students — before, during, or after class — began with him and his ideas and, sooner or later, returned to him and his ideas. He always remained at the center.

From Counterculture to Counterrevolution

At the end of the 1970s, Abbot saw all around him an academic society that behaved as though the 1960s had never happened. The reforms in teaching and learning that had taken place on his campus during the preceding decade had been eradicated quietly and without notice. Certain overt changes had been made democratically, of course, because his campus was noted for democratic governance. But the development was so pervasive, and the elimination of the reforms of the 1960s had been accomplished so smoothly, that Abbot was convinced there could be only one explanation: conspiracy and counter-revolution.

The academic revolution of the 1960s had been noisy and bloody, but the counterrevolution of the 1970s had taken place so quietly that no one knew about it until it had been accomplished. The conspiracy, Abbot felt, had started with the conservative faculty (which is to say, the majority of the faculty) and their administrative officers. Joining with them were powerful outside forces: the accrediting agencies, the disciplinary organizations and learned societies, and above all the controllers of the sources of funds — boards, government agencies, and state legislatures. Strengthened and encouraged by the business world and the professions — and by the new breed of students who would be seeking success in those areas — this powerful alliance of reactionary forces, Abbot believed, had launched a counterrevolution which, at the time of Nixon's resignation from the presidency, had reversed the direction of teaching and learning in the American university.

But there was another aspect of the whole situation that seemed even worse to Abbot. He came to the conclusion that, by not opposing the reactionary trend in education, by yielding to the pressures that pushed for a change away from a student-centered mode, he had himself unwillingly joined the counterrevolution. In fact, he felt tricked — much as, according to Millett's argument in *Sexual Politics* (1970), admirers of D. H. Lawrence, Henry Miller, and Norman Mailer were tricked into supporting the sexual counterrevolution when they believed they were supporting the liberation movement. Abbot realized that some observers denied there was either a counterrevolution or revolution. The curricular changes of the 1960s were surface changes only; as soon as reformers turned their attention to other matters, the system simply rejected the changes, reinstituting the old and more comfortable structures.

However accurate Abbot's interpretation of developments in higher education was, it was certain that in two tumultuous decades, he had gone through four distinct stages of development as a college teacher. Though it was not a subject many of his colleagues were interested in discussing, Abbot saw in most of them indications of similar changes and adaptations. Thinking back, Abbot concluded that his general style when he first began teaching was similar to the style of most of the professors who had taught him literature during his under-graduate years. When his style changed to more student-centered, more holistic modes, in the 1960s, so did the styles of many of his closer colleagues. And as they had adapted to changing conditions of the 1960s, so were most of them now adapting to the prevailing academic conditions of the late 1970s.

If he found a difference between himself and his colleagues in the present climate, it was that his observations about teaching style and educational aims troubled him greatly. He knew, no more than they, the right teaching style. He suspected that his own changing style was, in some small part, a result of conscious choice and effort and, in large part, an adaptation to circumstance. But that element of con-scious choice and effort, however small it might be, mattered—in the measures of satisfactions it afforded him as a teacher, in the guesses he made about what students were learning, and in the possible conse-quences of both to some seldom-voiced ideals that had led him to teach-ing in the first place.

When the year 1984 arrives, Abbot will have completed his twen-ty-fifth year of college teaching. How will things go between now and then? When that question is put to him, Abbot quietly sighs and shakes his head. He says only that he is not optimistic.

References

Axelrod, J., and others. *Search for Relevance.* San Francisco: Jossey-Bass, 1969.

Axelrod, J. *The University Teacher as Artist.* San Francisco: Jossey-Bass, 1973.

Carmichael, O. C. *Graduate Education: A Critique and a Program.* New York: Harper, 1961.

Henderson, A. D. *Policies and Practices in Higher Education.* New York: Harper, 1960.

Kerr, C. *The Uses of the University.* Cambridge, Mass.: Harvard University Press, 1963.

McGrath, E. J. *Liberal Education in the Professions.* New York: Teacher's College, Colum-bia University, 1959.

Medsker, L. L. *The Junior College: Progress and Prospect.* New York: McGraw-Hill, 1960.

Millet, K. *Sexual Politics.* New York: Doubleday, 1970.

Riesman, D. Quoted in M. L. Habein (Ed.), *Spotlight on the College Student.* Washing-ton, D.C.: American Council on Education, 1959.

Sanford, N. *The American College.* New York: Wiley, 1962.

Joseph Axelrod is professor of comparative literature and chairman of the department, California State University, San Francisco. A staff member of the Center for Research and Development in Higher Education, Berkeley, he directed a research project on model building for undergraduate colleges which led to his book The University Teacher as Artist: Toward an Aesthetics of Teaching with Emphasis on the Humanities *(Jossey-Bass, 1973).*

Graduate teaching assistants can be helped to develop
effective teaching styles by acquiring basic skills and
developing personality and character traits.

Conscious Teaching: Helping Graduate Assistants Develop Teaching Styles

John T. Granrose

Several years ago I decided to try to learn to play the banjo. I failed. Perhaps if I had really decided to learn, instead of just to *try,* I might have succeeded. In any case, I went to an excellent banjo player for lessons. During each of these lessons, he would play several banjo pieces for me, always at full speed. He also told stories of the days when he was first learning to play the banjo himself and urged me to practice hard between lessons. What he did not do — could not do, as it turned out — was to slow down his playing enough for me to learn how he made the wonderful sounds he did with the instrument. Nor could he talk clearly about what he was doing. His knowledge of the banjo was in his fingers. Now that is probably the best place for a banjo player's knowledge to be; with a banjo *teacher,* however, things are different. A banjo teacher — any teacher — needs to be consciously aware of what he or she is doing. Mine was not, and so I eventually gave up. But I did learn something about teaching.

It was Socrates, of course, who maintained that the unexamined life is not worth living. One need not be a philosophy teacher, however, to share the similar opinion that unexamined teaching is unworthy of a human being. (And quite apart from the moral issue of its "worthiness," it also does not appear to work very well when it comes to training new teachers.) But examining one's own teaching is a difficult enterprise, especially for graduate teaching assistants who are typically subject to intense pressures and anxieties of their own as graduate students. Starting several years ago I undertook the project of attempting to help a group of teaching assistants in philosophy reflect on college teaching generally and begin to form their own style of teaching. My concern for graduate assistants developed out of my own experience as a student and a beginning teacher.

I have been concerned (some might say "obsessed") with the problems of teaching ever since my days in high school. With one or two exceptions, my teachers at that time impressed me consistently as dull and uninteresting. This was true in spite of the fact that I was developing strong interests in several of their subjects. As a result of these experiences, I began my undergraduate studies with a very low opinion of teachers in general and with a total lack of interest in becoming a teacher myself. As an undergraduate and graduate student, however, something remarkable happened. I began more and more to encounter teachers who were alive to both their subject matter and their students, and whose bearing and conversation revealed a depth of experience that I admired. While these admired teachers were always a minority of the faculty members with whom I came into contact, I began to see the possibilities of inspired teaching, and I came to know firsthand the kind of influence such teachers could have on a student. I began to wonder how these inspiring teachers came to be the way they were and why there were not more like them. As my own interests shifted toward teaching I vowed that if I should ever become a teacher I would search for the secret of the inspired teaching which I had so admired.

During my own career as a graduate teaching assistant, I found myself thrust into the classroom with little preparation except in my subject matter. What meetings there were between teaching fellows and faculty members were limited largely to discussions of the fine points in the assigned readings and issues connected with grading the tests. But, as before, I was too shy to ask for any extra help or advice. What I did instead was to read everything I could find about college teaching and its improvement. Among the books I read during that anxious time the early 1960s were Jacques Barzun's *Teacher in America* (1954), Gilbert Highet's *Art of Teaching* (1950), and Wilbert McKeachie's *Teaching Tips* (1951). While these books were helpful in some ways, I had a difficult time making full use of their insights — perhaps because there was no one with whom I could discuss my thoughts about them. For the most part I simply muddled through my years as a beginning teacher. At that point, however, I made a second vow — the vow that I would do what I could to help other beginning teachers if I ever got to the point where I had something to offer them. This chapter describes some of the steps I have taken towards fulfilling these two vows. The whole point is to bring some skills and attitudes connected with teaching into conscious focus so that they may be examined.

Style and Teaching

Of the twenty-five to thirty graduate students in philosophy at the University of Georgia each year, about a dozen ordinarily serve as teaching assistants. Several years ago, the department as a whole decided to try to help these new teachers and their undergraduate students in two ways. First, it was made a matter of department policy that no graduate teaching assistant could teach his or her own course without having first assisted (and been supervised by) a regular faculty member in that course. Second, an ongoing discussion group of teaching assistants and other interested graduate students was formed. This group met every two weeks during the entire academic year, ordinarily either for lunch or for late afternoon refreshments, in one of the several restaurants adjacent to our campus. (The department was able to obtain a small grant to pay for the food and drink at these meetings.) In preparation for each of our bi-weekly gatherings, we read a chapter in Kenneth Eble's *The Craft of Teaching: A Guide to Mastering the Professor's Art* (1976). The sixteen chapters of Eble's book blend together a philosophy of teaching and some practical advice about such skills as lecturing, leading discussions, selecting texts, and grading. These discussions were always lively, sometimes heated, and generally "consciousness raising." Although we did not articulate it in these terms at the time, the overall purpose of this project was to help new and prospective instructors develop and examine their own teaching styles.

Style, according to the *New Columbia Encyclopedia,* is "the mysterious yet recognizable result of a successful blending of form with content." The content in the present instance is, of course, some part of the discipline of philosophy, although it could be any of the other humanities, the social sciences, or the physical sciences as well. The form, however, which embodies this content may be thought of in two ways. Perhaps the most obvious of these is the course itself: the text, the syllabus, the tests, and the like. Another way of embodying this content, however, is in the personality of the teacher himself or herself. It is this sense of form which seems to me most fundamental here.

There is a striking passage in the *Bhagavad-Gita* in which Arjuna asks Krishna about the marks of an enlightened person: "In what manner does an illumined soul speak: How does he sit? How does he walk?" What Arjuna's questions suggest to me is that enlightenment or "illumination" is a matter of what might be called personal "wholeness," rather than simply the possession of certain skills, beliefs, or attitudes.

Basic Skills of Teaching

Highet (1950), McKeachie (1979), and Eble (1976) all discuss certain basic skills of teaching. My own way of conceptualizing these skills, which has emerged from my work with graduate teaching assistants, differs from theirs in several ways. Some of these differences should emerge from the following discussions of what I consider the basic skills of teaching: *choosing, preparing, speaking, listening, responding, testing,* and *grading*. (Taken together, these basic skills might be labeled, in theological terms, "the lesser mysteries.")

Choosing. Before a class has begun there are many choices to be made.. The choice of a textbook, for example, is one of the most influential acts in teaching. (In my department at the University of Georgia graduate teaching assistants are free to choose their own textbooks for the courses they teach. I gather that this practice is widespread, although not universal.) In some cases, depending on the flexibility and the democracy in a given department, there may be the still more fundamental choice of which course to teach or the choice of subject matter to be included under a rather general course title. Once the class has begun there are still further choices to be made regarding class format and assignments, in addition to the obvious choices connected with the following more specific basic skills. One need not be an existentialist to affirm that one's choices reveal and shape one's basic style, and indeed, who one is.

Preparing. Does it go without saying that teachers should be prepared to teach the whole of their courses and to teach each specific class? Teachers, however, like everyone else, face temptations not to do what they know they should. In the case of choosing, the most pressing moral temptation is to try to evade one's responsibility, either by pretending that the opportunity to choose does not exist (or that one's options are far narrower than they are in reality) or to simply make hasty or ill-formed choices. In the case of preparation, the primary danger seems to be the temptation to cut corners. (This temptation also exists, perhaps even more notoriously, when it comes to testing and grading.) No good teacher ought to agonize over whether he or she ought to prepare for his or her classes. Surely this is one of the most elementary professional obligations. To accept this, of course, does nothing to answer the question of how much preparation is actually needed. That may be one of those questions to which no helpful answer can be given — except to point out that careful attention to one's experiences in class will provide evidence when one is underprepared.

It may also be worth noting that the obligation to be prepared for class is what philosophers call a *prima facie* obligation; that is, an obligation which holds, other things being equal. Although *prima facie* obligations may be overridden by other obligations on occasion, when there are no conflicts they always apply. An example of this would be the obligation to take an injured child to the hospital overriding the obligation to prepare for a particular class whenever these two obligations come into conflict. Other things being equal, however, adequate preparation is simply obligatory. But preparation involves work and time, and since there are many conflicting demands on the time and energy of graduate teaching assistants, it is clear why there may be strong temptations to cut corners here. To point out these temptations and discuss them freely with beginning graduate assistants has, I believe, helped them develop teaching styles which are honest and straightforward.

Speaking. It is one thing to advise a beginning teacher simply to "speak clearly." It is quite another, however, to explain what clearness of speech is and how to achieve it. Even those who exemplify it may find these tasks of explanation difficult (as did the banjo teacher I mentioned earlier). At the very least, a division between the phonetic and structural aspects of speaking clearly may be helpful.

During my years as a student I had several teachers who had difficulty speaking so that their words could be heard and understood. But it was not until I began working with beginning teachers that I realized how widespread such problems could be. As the advisor and supervisor of the graduate teaching assistants in our department, I routinely read the evaluation questionnaires which are completed by all students in their courses. As many as a fourth of these beginning teachers have been accused by their students of mumbling, speaking too softly or speaking in a monotone. For the most part, these speech problems have proved correctable — although the problem of speaking in a monotone seems to be somewhat more deeply rooted. The first step, as usual, is to become conscious of the problem.

What I have referred to as "structural" problems in clear speaking appear to be more difficult to overcome. Under structural issues I include not merely the inability of some beginning teachers to speak in complete, grammatical sentences, but also general problems in the flow, pattern, and organization of what is said. The absence, vagueness, or incoherence of structure in a lecture would, no doubt, be generally considered a defect. (It should be perhaps added that such defects, like the obligations cited earlier, might appropriately be labeled *prima facie* defects. It seems conceivable that such defects might be overcome or overridden in particular situations just as obligations may be.)

A related problem to which beginning teachers are particularly

prone (although we all doubtless know experienced teachers who suc-
cumb to this as well) is an overuse of fancy words or jargon. Since
Strunk and White, in *The Elements of Style* (1979), and Trilling, in *Sincerity and Authenticity* (1972) and in his other works, have so strongly criti-
cized this academic form of affectation, I need do no more than men-
tion it as a reminder.

Listening. Admonitions about listening are as old as the Bible
("he who has ears to hear, let him hear,"), and as recent as contemporary courses on such topics as "Active Listening" and "Listening Skills
for Business Executives." The truth of the matter is that listening well is
a skill which many of us must take special pains to acquire. Paying
attention, of course, is a necessary condition for listening (just as it is
for remembering names and faces, for example). But I am convinced
that listening well also involves *caring,* both about the speaker and
about the subject under discussion. For this reason it requires the
development of a certain type of character, a topic to which I shall
return. Furthermore, accurate listening typically requires a background of general and specific knowledge — in other words, a context.
There is, unfortunately, no shortcut to developing this background.
Just as a willingness to work hard is an essential part of preparing for
class, energy and hard work may be required to develop the general
and specific knowledge that will aid in listening well. On the other
hand, however, since graduate teaching assistants are generally closer
in age to the students they teach than faculty members are, and hence
may share more common background knowledge with their students,
they may have an advantage in this area even without any extra effort.

Perhaps the most helpful general advice here would be that
teachers, whether graduate assistants or faculty members, regularly
ask themselves whether they are giving their students sufficient opportunity to question or comment and then remind themselves to try to listen well to what these students say.

Responding. Having listened carefully to a student, how does
one respond? Aristotle's advice about choosing the path between ex remes
is relevant here. The one extreme is based on the strong temptation
which most of us occasionally feel to respond defensively to student comments and questions. A catalog of the many ways in which teacher
responses may be defensive would roughly parallel the traditional classification of Freudian defense mechanisms. (I once spoke with a well-
known poet at a conference on improving teaching. The only general
advice that he could give us about improving as teachers was to go
through psychotherapy.) Rather than responding defensively to students, the thing to do seems to be to respond appropriately, and even
generously. But the key to overcoming our defensiveness, according to
traditional theories of psychotherapy, is to become conscious of what we
are doing — "conscious teaching." Generosity in one's responses can also

be carried to extremes, however. While a generous response will not directly undermine a student's self-esteem or motivation to participate in class, a generosity which leads the teacher to completely overlook error or ambiguity in student comments will severely limit the intellectual gains which are likely in a course.

Some teachers have a tendency to err one way; others err in the opposite direction. Here again, Aristotle (1974) has some appropriate advice to offer. Once we have discovered the mistakes to which we are particularly prone, "we must drag ourselves in the opposite direction to them; for it is by removing ourselves as far as possible from what is wrong that we shall arrive at the mean, as we do when we pull a crooked stick straight" (p. 244).

One further point must be made here. A sense of timing is of critical importance in teaching, especially in those acts which are here referred to as "responding." A crucial first step for an educator is the building of each student's self-confidence in relation to the subject matter and trust in the teacher. Once a basic level of trust and rapport has been established, the time for challenging and confronting students will come. Judging just when that time has come is a sensitive issue. The development of a sense of timing in teaching, as in the other arts, seems to benefit from coaching, the emulation of models, and trial-and-error experience. A sense of "rhythm" must be developed, a rhythm similar to that referred to by Whitehead (1929) in has chapter "The Rhythmic Claims of Freedom and Discipline" in *The Aims of Education.*

Testing and Grading. While testing and grading typically take place at several points during a course, they nearly always take place at the conclusion of a course, and so this topic will conclude the examination of basic skills in teaching. The several books of advice on teaching which I have mentioned contain detailed discussions of both topics. Also, in contrast to such topics as lecturing and leading discussions, graduate students will often have reflected on standards of fairness and appropriateness in testing and grading throughout their careers as students. And *Change Magazine* has published a long policy paper to which new teachers can be referred: *The Testing and Grading of Students,* (Milton and Edgerly, 1976). What new teachers need, it seems to me, is a chance — and a mandate — to discuss what they read and think on this important topic. (I recall Cardinal Newman's observation that the purpose of a university is not to *read* books, but to discuss them and the world of ideas in which they exist.)

Advanced Skills of Teaching

The skills which have been discussed thus far are merely the basics of teaching. They are the marks of competence and craftsmanship in one's profession. They help create a teacher's style. But they do not define style nor do they play the crucial part in developing a style. For this we must turn to "advanced skills" which seem to be necessary for "inspired" teaching. The skills and attitudes involved in such teaching might correspond to what theologians call "the greater mysteries." One reason that these advanced skills receive relatively little attention in works on teaching is that they are difficult, sometimes embarrassing, to talk about.

Many years ago I heard Robert Frost remark that when he bought a new book he left it on his bookshelf for several years so that he could read and meditate on the title on its spine. He claimed that he usually found thinking about the title more helpful than reading the book itself. While I am generally more receptive to the content of books than Frost claimed to have been, I too find meditation on book titles frequently provocative. One such title belongs to a book which I have recently used in my philosophy classes: *Coming of Age in Philosophy* by Roger Eastman (1973). Images such as "coming of age," "growing up," or "awakening" strike me as very close to the heart of what inspired teaching is about. So, too, in the preparation of new teachers one would expect such images to apply. If these images are anywhere close to the mark, it becomes understandable why the preparation of graduate students to become college teachers is such a difficult business. Growing up, after all, simply takes time as well as a certain sort of nurturing attention. These facts loomed large for the ancient Greeks who generally thought that persons below the age of thir y-five or forty were unfit to study philosophy, let alone to teach it.

American philosopher Josiah Royce, however, provides greater insight into the process of growing up and its relation to teaching. In *The Religious Aspects of Philosophy* (1885) Royce points out the inevitability of total selfishness in infants and small children. In fact, claims Royce, we care at first only about our own *present* pleasures and pains. Eventually, however, our horizons broaden to include the pleasures and pains which may come to us in the future. This dawning awareness of our "future self" becomes the foundation for the virtue called "prudence." At first our future self is unreal to us. It is a ghost and nothing more. In a similar fashion, says Royce, even after we have developed a sense of prudence about our future, a further step is necessary in order to grow up morally. This necessary step is the recognition that other persons are real, that they know fears, hopes, and dreams just as we do. In Royce's (1958) old fashioned language: ". . . thy neighbor is as actual, as concrete, as thou art. Just as thy future is real, though not now thine, so thy neighbor is real, though his thoughts are never thy thoughts. Dost thou believe this? Art thou sure what it means? This is for thee the turning point of thy whole conduct toward him" (p. 157).

Once we have achieved this moral insight (which Royce distinguishes from a mere feeling such as a "gush of pity"), we naturally resolve to treat our neighbor as real, that is, to show him or her the same respect and consideration we would ourselves. Royce, however, is somewhat pessimistic (although not cynical) about our chances of complete success in this undertaking. Our passions frequently lead us to forget this insight even after it has been achieved. "Moments of insight, with their accompanying resolutions; long stretches of delusion and selfishness: That is our life," (p. 156) writes Royce. This awareness of the inevitability of human forgetfulness, weakness, backsliding, or sin is a striking contrast to much of modern moral philosophy. His view rings true to me.

If Royce's view of human development is correct, and if growing up naturally involves the realization that other people are real and the resolution to treat them as such, we have here a philosophical theory with major implications for teachers.

Gilbert Highet (1950) spoke of "liking the pupils" as one of the qualities of a good teacher. I agree that, other things being equal at least, it is useful if one likes one's students. To be inspiring as a teacher, however, it is far more useful if one loves and respects one's students, rather than simply "liking" them. ("Loving" and "respecting" are not as closely tied to a particular feeling or sensation as "liking" is.) I recall a passage in which Jeremy Bentham suggested that the way to be comfortable was to make others comfortable, the way to make others comfortable was to appear to love them, and the way to appear to love them was to love them in reality. Something like this, I am convinced, is a necessary part of the best teaching. To love someone in this way involves Royce's calm, clear insight and a conscious commitment to that person's welfare — not what Royce refers to as a "gush of pity" or a "tremulous weakness of sympathy."

Supposing then that we were serious about such an approach to developing a teaching style, how would we learn to love our students in this way? Not primarily, surely, by reading books on the subject, although books may provide us with some important clues. The primary way in which we learn to love them, I believe, is by first being loved ourselves and then sharing with them what we ourselves have experienced. While this cannot be proved, I am convinced that such love leaves its imprint on our total character and style of living. After all, to wake our students up, we ourselves must be awake; to inspire them, we ourselves must be inspired; to love them, we must be loved ourselves. Such, at least, is the faith on which I have based my approach to teaching and to helping graduate students develop into teachers.

To blend form and content into a successful style of teaching is fundamentally a question of developing a certain wholeness of character from which the details of one's teaching will flow. As Nietzsche wrote: "Giving style to one's character—a great and rare art!" It is not easy, but perhaps we can love and help each other along the way.

References

Aristotle. *The Nichomachean Ethics of Aristotle.* London: Macmillan, 1892. In W. K. Frankena and J. T. Granrose (Eds.), *Introductory Readings in Ethics.* Englewood Cliffs, N.J.: Prentice-Hall, 1974.

Barzun, J. *Teacher in America.* New York: Doubleday, 1954.

Bhagavad-Gita. In W. K. Frankena and J. T. Granrose (Eds.), *Introductory Readings in Ethics.* Englewood Cliffs, N.J.: Prentice-Hall, 1974.

Eastman, R. *Coming of Age in Philosophy.* San Francisco: Canfield Press, 1973.

Eble, K. *The Craft of Teaching: A Guide to Mastering the Professor's Art.* San Francisco: Jossey-Bass, 1976.

Highet, G. *The Art of Teaching.* New York: Knopf, 1950.

McKeachie, W. *Teaching Tips: A Guidebook for the Beginning College Teacher.* Lexington, Mass.: Heath, 1979.

Milton, O., and Edgerly, J. *The Testing and Grading of Students.* New Rochelle, N.Y.: *Change Magazine,* 1976.

Nietzsche, F. *The Gay Science.* In W. Kaufmann (Ed.), *The Portable Nietzsche.* New York: Viking, 1954.

Royce, J. *The Religious Aspect of Philosophy.* New York: Harper, 1958.

Strunk, W., and White, E. B. *The Elements of Style.* (3rd ed.) New York: Macmillan, 1979.

Trilling, L. *Sincerity and Authority.* Cambridge, Mass.: Harvard, 1972.

Whitehead, A. *The Aims of Education.* New York: Macmillan, 1929.

John T. Granrose teaches philosophy at the University of Georgia. He is a Danforth Associate, and a small grant from the Danforth Foundation's College Project Fund enabled him to conduct the special kind of development program for graduate teaching assistants reported on here.

Changing one's teaching style involves a careful analysis of one's own and one's students' needs; the teaching strategies adopted must serve both.

The Teacher as Leader

Edward Glassman

About five years ago, after years of moderate success as a university teacher of biochemistry and genetics, I made a discovery that has affected my teaching ever since. I realized that when I lectured I was the one who learned most. I was the one whose thinking skills were enhanced and whose creativity was stimulated. I played the active learning role; the students' role was passive, often consisting of listening and trying to decipher what I was trying to say during the lecture.

As a result, I changed my style of teaching radically with beneficial consequences to both myself and my students. The beginning of that change was an honest confronting and clarifying of my goals in teaching. Though my goals differed somewhat from course to course, the main pattern of objectives with respect both to students and myself was clear and consistent. I set them down in writing this way:

> For my students, my goals are to make them aware of the subject matter, to enable them to learn and remember lots of content. I want to enhance thinking skills, to stimulate creativity, and to develop self-motivation and self-directed learning skills; to create in them a need to know the content, rather than

I am grateful to Professor Eugene R. Watson of the Division of Higher and Adult Education of the School of Education and of the University of North Carolina at Chapel Hill for sharing his ideas and expertise with me in his courses, in conversations, and in workshops.

coercing them to learn. I want them to have a positive attitude toward each other, toward the subject matter, and toward me.

For myself, my goals are to achieve the above and at the same time to provide for myself more time to spend on research, scholarship, and other academic activities without slighting the needs of my students.

Having clarified my goals, I set about examining alternative teaching styles, ways of improving the students' command of content, of stimulating individual creativity, and of enhancing thinking skills. One important disco ery was that many organization development consultants shared my views about lecturing and had developed ways to achieve my goals through the use of groups engaged in cooperative experiential learning. I discovered that the extensive leadership theory developed for other organizations could be productively applied to my own teaching. Teachers are leaders, and leadership theory* has productive applications to achieving teaching goals through appropriate teacher behaviors.

In this chapter, I shall first state the leadership theory that I think most relates to my classroom, and then apply this theory to three teaching formats I use — lecturing, discussion groups, and cooperative learning groups. Those aspects of current leadership theory that seem most pertinent to my teaching are:

1. Leadership is defined by a set of behaviors and skills, not necessarily by traits possessed by an individual.

2. Leaders are trained, not born, and although part of the training has taken place in early life, adults can be trained to be effective leaders.

3. Qualities in leader behavior that seem to be very important are:
   a. the degree of control the leader exerts over followers (directive, non-directive, and participative styles)
   b. the amount of support a leader provides to followers (supportive *vs.* non-supportive styles)
   c. the skills and judgment when to do the above (effective *vs.* ineffective styles).

4. Some effective leader behaviors go with various leader styles: telling, asserting behavior (directive style); negotiating behavior (participative style); facilitating, encouraging or delegating behavior (non-directive style). Their ineffective behavioral counterparts might be perceived by subordinates

*These ideas are derived from Hershey and Blanchard (1977), Lassey and Fernandez (1976), Moore (1976), and Reddin (1970).

as: dictating or over-protecting behavior (directive style); compromising behavior (participative style); and permissive, soft-hearted, or passive behavior (non-directive style).

5. The criteria of when to use a particular leader behavior depends on:
   a. the goals of the leader
   b. the level of skills the leader has for each behavior
   c. the ability of the followers
   d. the situation, the importance, and difficulty of the task
   e. the time available
   f. the expertise of the leader
   g. the availability of resources other than those of the leader.

The accompanying table applies these ideas about leader styles and behaviors to the classroom.

Which style is best in teaching? In general, the most effective leaders are those who have the flexibility to use the appropriate style and behaviors called for in a given situation, or those whose style and behaviors match most of the situations encountered in their work. Thus, teachers need to choose those behaviors that are apporpriate to achieving their goals.

The communication skills required for these leader behaviors are described in detail elsewhere. I find Gordon (1974) very valuable for learning about the *asserting* skill of using I-messages, the skills for no-lose *negotiating,* and the *facilitating* skill of active listening. Some *asserting* skills are persistence, reacting non-defensively to criticism, admitting errors and mistakes, self-disclosure, and soliciting and accepting feedback. Smith (1975) gives very useful guidance here. Bergquist, Phillips, and Quehl (1975) usefully describe the *facilitating* skill of paraphrasing and the *asserting* skill of giving feedback. Rogers (1969), Gordon (1974), and Knowles (1975) provide important discussions concerning the skills and attitudes of *delegating* and *modeling.* These are not the only sources that describe these skills, but are the ones that were particularly useful for me.

In the sections that follow, I shall describe how I apply this theoretical description of leader behaviors and skills to my own teaching.

Lecturing

When lecturing is the chosen format, it is important to attempt to achieve my goal of enhancing thinking skills and stimulating creativity, even though the lecture hall is large and the time available prevents extensive group discussion.

I introduce content through guided reading assignments as well

Table 1. The Effect of Various Leader Styles and Behaviors on Learning Goals in the Classroom

Leader Style:	Directive	Participative	Non-Directive
Leader Behavior:	Telling; Asserting; Modeling	Negotiating	Delegating; Consulting; Facilitating
Teaching Style:	Instructor-Centered	Person-Centered	Student-Centered
Some Common Formats:	Lecturing; Personalized System of Instruction Lecturing (P.S.I.); Self-instructional packages; some teacher-led discussion groups; competency-based courses	Some teacher-led discussion groups	Cooperative learning groups; self-directed learning contracts
Learning Objectives (Bloom, and others, 1956): Knowledge and Comprehension	In this style, knowledge comes the teacher, little or none from the student; yet if done well can be an effective way to disseminate knowledge.	Most effective use of human resources in the classroom when knowledge comes from the teacher and students.	Knowledge comes from the students. The teacher's expertise is not used and may be lost if special efforts are not made by all concerned.
Application and Analysis and Synthesis	Using these leader behaviors, creative expression comes from the teacher. Students are not likely to be creative or to express creative ideas when these leader behaviors dominate a classroom or a course.	Both the teacher and the students are given a chance to *express* creative thoughts leading to an enhancement of thinking skills and creativity of all persons in the classroom.	Greatest opportunity for a student to *enhance* thinking skills and stimulate creativity is when the teacher facilitates and encourages but does not participate.
Evaluation	Ability to learn and develop these skills is difficult for a student when the teacher is using these leader behaviors.	Greatest opportunity to *learn* evaluation skills comes during participative efforts of the students and the teacher.	Greatest opportunity to *develop* evaluation skills comes when the teacher encourages and delegates, but does not participate.

as through lectures, and I attempt to enhance creativity and thinking skills through buzz groups. To form these, I ask the students to turn in their seats and form groups of five persons. I then ask the buzz groups to do one of the following: 1) clarify confusing parts of a reading assignment or the lecture, 2) list questions everyone in the buzz group would like to have answered, 3) choose topics everyone in the buzz group would like to have pursued in the lecture and by other buzz groups. In other words, I move back and forth from telling behavior to delegating behavior during a lecture.

For example, if this chapter were to be delivered in lecture form, I would stop after describing my goals, and ask members of a buzz group to share teaching goals with one another. After presenting the leadership theory, I would ask them to share what leader behaviors they want to develop in order to achieve their goals. After the section on skills, I would ask them to identify the skills they need to develop the leader behaviors, and how they would develop these skills. After this section on lecturing, I would ask them to discuss the teaching formats they now use, whether these teaching formats help them achieve their goals, and what formats they would like to use in the future. Finally, at the end of the lecture, I would ask each person to list questions he or she wanted answered. I would then ask each buzz group to answer whatever questions could be answered within the group and to pass those questions to me that everyone in the group would like answered. This helps to screen the questions I am asked, and I am also assured that at least the five people in the buzz group want to listen to me talk on that particular aspect of The Teacher as Leader.

Leading Discussion Groups

The teacher as leader has important challenges when leading a discussion group. This is where leader behaviors most clearly affect outcomes. Figure 1 shows four communication patterns I have observed in teacher-led discussion groups. Pattern A occurs mostly when a teacher using directive teaching styles (telling and asserting behaviors) is introducing content or new ideas into the group or asking questions. The pattern consists of the teacher talking, a student talking, the teacher talking, and so on in this pattern, the facts, ideas, thinking and creativity usually belong to the teacher. Students rarely contribute creatively in such a discussion.

In order to get students to contribute, the teacher often uses a nondirective teaching style and stops talking in hopes that Pattern C will emerge; that is, all students contributing facts, ideas, creativity, and thinking to the discussion to help the group achieve its learning goals. In point of fact, Pattern D most often emerges when a teacher

Figure 1. Some Common Communication Patterns in
Instructor-Led Discussion Groups

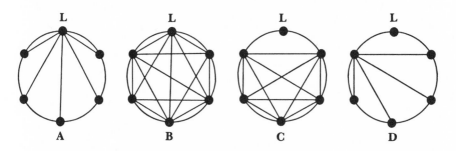

stops talking. Here one or more students plays the role of directive teacher. My goal in leading discussion groups is to achieve Pattern B — a person-centered, participative discussion in which all persons contribute facts, ideas, notions, theories, thinking, and creativity as needed to accomplish the learning goals of the group.

This is achievable when the faculty and the students use effective group discussion skills, cooperate instead of compete, and use techniques for productive group discussion. These techniques include separating creative, evaluative, and analytic thinking modes from each other, and using force field analysis, brainstorming, nominal group process, census, and consensus negotiation to make decisions.

A single leader behavior is seldom suitable for every stage of a discussion-centered course. Customarily, I use various leader behaviors depending on the stage of development of the discussion group. For example, with a new discussion group (Stage 1), my goal is to make them aware of course content and effective group discussion skills. Therefore, I use mainly telling and asserting leader behavior: I choose the content; I train the group; and I design and lead the session, assign guided reading assignments, generate the discussion topics, decide grading methods, and the like.

In Stage 2 the discussion group is aware of content and discussion skills, and my goal is to encourage them to participate in discussions with me (Pattern B, Figure 1). To accomplish this I use negotiating behavior combined with asserting and facilitating behavior. The group and I negotiate content, process, learning contracts, grading, and other important aspects of the course.

In Stage 3 the discussion group has good discussion skills and is learning and cooperating well in discussions. My goal is to let go of the leadership. I therefore use facilitating and delegating leader behaviors. I listen and support the discussion group in its effort to learn through discussion.

In Stage 4 the discussion group is cooperative and sophisticated — the group members have good learning and discussion skills; they plan and learn together effectively. My goal is to encourage them to continue and for me to join the group as an equal. To accomplish this I use delegating leader behavior much of the time; this enables me to participate as a member of the discussion group as shown in Pattern B (Figure 1). It seems the more I delegate at this stage, the more I can contribute without producing Pattern A (Figure 1). Moving through the Cycle of Leadership Styles (Figure 2) with careful, deliberate intent is one way a teacher can achieve a person-centered, participative discussion group (Pattern B, Figure 1).

Cooperative Learning Groups

> We trained hard . . . but it seemed that every time we were beginning to form teams we would be reorganized. . . . I was to learn later in life that we tend to meet any new situation by reorganizing, and a wonderful method it can be for creating the illusion of progress while producing confusion, inefficiency and demoralization.
>
> Petronius Arbiter (210 BC)

The teaching method that has excited me most in enabling me to achieve the sometimes conflicting goals I had set for myself and my students is the use of the Cooperative Learning Group (Glassman, 1978). This is a permanently formed, relatively independent group of eight to ten students. In this approach I initially accept responsibility for focusing and structuring the learning experience, and the students accept and share responsibility for actively pursuing their own learning.

The following partially describes the role of the faculty in this format:

1. The faculty *are not members* of the learning group and do not sit with the learning group except by negotiation, and then for the minimum amount of time necessary to accomplish the agenda agreed upon.

2. The faculty *attend to their goals* and needs in the course; the learning group attends to theirs. If there is a conflict between the goals and needs of the faculty and the learning group, such conflicts are resolved by negotiation using systematic group discussion techniques that facilitate the achievement of consensus. It is desirable that the faculty and the student group are trained in the use of these techniques.

3. The faculty *set limits* for the learning group consistent with their own goals and needs, with the goals and needs of other relevant faculty, and with the goals and needs of the institution. These limits

involve course objectives, scheduling, exams, grades, and so forth, although these may be open for negotiation with the learning group when feasible.

4. The faculty *introduce content* through guided reading assignments, structured exercises, discussion questions, lecturettes, study guides, problems to be solved, and the like. The use of guided reading assignments is an effective alternative to lectures as a means of introducing content.

5. The faculty *are mainly resource consultants* to the learning group. As such, the faculty avoid answering most questions and giving opinions pertaining to content (so they are not perceived by the students as the only experts present); avoid judging and evaluating student achievement prematurely (and thus allow students to risk and then learn from their own mistakes); avoid being totally responsible for what the student learns in the course (and thus place the responsibility for learning on the student); avoid being the sole sources of student motivation (and thereby allow self-motivation and self-direction to occur).

6. The faculty member *is a guide to the processes* of group discussion that facilitate creativity, independence, and self-direction in the learning group. Through short exercises and questionnaires designed to increase awareness of helpful and dysfunctional activities in groups that affect learning, group members are trained in group discussion skills that lead to cooperative interactions that facilitate the learning process in each student.

Thus, the learning group format is not faculty-oriented, student-oriented, or group-oriented. It is person-oriented, and can be organized to meet most needs of the faculty, the students, and the learning group through negotiation and consensus decision making. This format asserts the independence and the options of all participants in the course.

The leader behaviors that I use with Cooperative Learning Groups vary with my goals and with the level of abilities of the learning group with respect to group discussion skills, knowledge of content, and ability to arrange productive learning experiences for themselves. I use the Cycle of Leader Behaviors similar to the one I described for Discussion Groups (Figure 2).

At the beginning, I use mainly telling and assertive behavior. I choose the content, I train the groups, I design the sessions, I provide guided reading assignments and discussion problems (Stage 1).

Once groups are aware of content and process, my goal is to enable them to start their own planning. Then I use negotiating behavior coupled with assertive and facilitative behavior. We negotiate content, process, learning contracts, and the like (Stage 2).

The next step is for the groups to become independent, so I use

Figure 2. A Cycle of Leader Behaviors in the Classroom

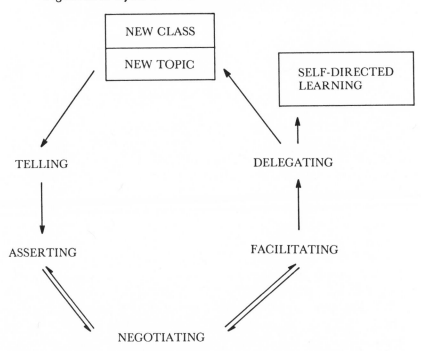

facilitative behavior combined with delegating behavior. I listen to and support groups in their efforts to learn and achieve (Stage 3).

The last step is to enable groups to remain independent. I use delegating behavior almost exclusively, combined with some negotiating behavior when appropriate. The groups are now self-directive (Stage 4).

I must emphasize that these last stages are not always achieved; nor do I find it desirable in some classes for the groups to move beyond Stages 2 or 3. In addition, groups move forward and backward, and teachers need to develop diagnosing skills to determine in what stage a group is operating in a particular session. My own style tends to lean towards facilitating and delegating behavior—my groups mature rapidly, but some students report a great deal of discomfort in early sessions. This may mean that their needs for dependence in early sessions are not met, and I probably do not use telling and assertive behavior enough with newly formed groups.

In comparing results from a class I taught in molecular and biochemical genetics as a lecture course and then later revised as one for a cooperative learning group, the differences were truly astounding to me. Although both courses were well received, the course taught for a cooperative learning group was noteworthy because of the enthusiasm and motivation of the students to learn content. Their attitude toward the subject matter was very positive—they really wanted to learn, and worked hard and interacted well to do so (Glassman, 1978).

Concluding Remarks

In reflecting on my own experience, I think a faculty member desiring to develop a new teaching style entailing different teaching behaviors might take the following steps:

- Clarify goals on teaching with respect to students and to one-self.
- Determine the teaching methods and instructional formats necessary to achieve these goals.
- Determine the leader behaviors needed for these formats.
- Determine the skills necessary to performing those behaviors more effectively, and decide how these skills can be developed.
- Attend appropriate workshops, courses, seminars, to develop those skills.

I do not know if this will work for everyone. Some faculty with whom I have shared this report that it has clarified their thinking and teaching, that they are developing the new skills that they have chosen, and that their teaching is becoming more effective.

References

Bergquist, W. H., Phillips, S. R., and Quehl, G. *A Handbook for Faculty Development.* Washington, D.C.: Council for the Advancement of Small Colleges, 1975.

Bloom, B. S. and others (Eds.). *Taxonomy of Educational Objectives—The Classification of Educational Goals, Handbook I: Cognitive Domains.* New York: David McKay, 1956.

Glassman, E. "Teaching Biochemistry in Cooperative Learning Groups." *Biochemical Education,* 1978, *6* (35).

Gordon, T. *T.E.T.: Teacher Effectiveness Training.* New York: Wyden, 1974.

Hershey, P., and Blanchard, K. *Management of Organizational Behavior.* Englewood Cliffs, N.J.: Prentice-Hall, 1977.

Knowles, M. *Self-Directed Learning.* New York: Association Press, 1975.

Lassey, W. R., and Fernandez, R. R. *Leadership and Social Change.* La Jolla, Calif.: University Associates, 1976.

Moore, L. I. "The FMI: Dimensions of Follower Maturity." *Group and Organization Studies,* 1976, *1* (2), 203–222.

Reddin, W. J. *Managerial Effectiveness.* New York: McGraw-Hill, 1970.

Rogers, C. R. *Freedom to Learn.* Columbia, Ohio: C. E. Merrill, 1969.

Smith, J. J. *When I Say No, I Feel Guilty.* New York: Bantam Books, 1975.

Edward Glassman is professor of biochemistry and genetics at the Medical School, University of North Carolina, Chapel Hill. He is also an educational consultant, most recently a consultant-in-residence and visiting professor in the School of Biological Sciences, University of California, Irvine.

Perceiving teaching as an interactive process leads to the adoption of teaching styles which draw upon the fund of research and experience with group processes of learning.

Teaching as an Interactive Process

Mary Lynn Crow

Like most university professors, I was a university student for many years. Most of my classes were concluded a few minutes before the bell—just in time for the professor to ask: "Are there any questions?" This was the "discussion" part of what was termed the lecture-discussion mode. To me those few minutes were often the most invigorating part of the entire class. Years later when I made the transition from student to professor, I considered a technique which would expand those last few minutes to the entire class period but which would not dilute the content or diminish the intellectual challenge. Realizing the attractiveness of finally being able to pass on the knowledge I had been amassing and the authority implicit in this posture, I nevertheless felt I had to confront the discrepancy between what felt comfortable to me as a teacher and what had felt comfortable to me as a learner. That confrontation opened the door to an exploration of my role as teacher and of my students' roles as learners.

In the main, a person's values, beliefs, and philosophy can easily be ascertained by the way he or she teaches. The instructional strategies and techniques that are adopted by a teacher bespeak his attitudes about himself, his students, and their respective roles in the teaching-learning process. They bespeak his belief about how people learn and therefore about the proper techniques one utilizes to help learning occur.

Style and Interactive Techniques

Instructors who begin to move to genuinely interactive discussion techniques quickly realize that these techniques oppose the traditional authority posture of the professor. The concern is valid. Group interaction techniques remove (if only temporarily) the professor from his role as primary information-giver and explainer. To adopt interaction strategies, a teacher must make some changes with respect to his psychological position toward both his subject matter and his students. Bolton and Boyer (1971), in describing the many differences between one-way (lecturing, for example) and two-way (interactive techniques) communication processes in the college classroom, note the psychological effect that occurs when a teacher engages in a group discussion activity. In this instance he relinquishes his "psychological bigness" and instead assumes a "psychological smallness." When the teacher is perceived as bigger than any of his students, students hesitate to speak up; they are reluctant to express opinions which might offend the teacher.

> When the teacher is psychologically big, students have a tendency to lean heavily upon him. They expect him to solve many problems, to see that all goes well, to take care of them. This can easily result in apathy, lack of initiative, and dependence. Another, less apparent consequence, is hidden resentment and frustration in those who are psychologically small. Believing they must carefully nurture the good will of the "big" leader they do not feel free to be themselves. They feel they must defer to him and, in a sense, deny their own individuality. Thus, even when the teacher is doing a good job of taking care of his students, considerable inner resentment may be building. Stated in psychological terms, conditions producing inappropriate dependency usually produce hidden frustration and hostility.
>
> The solution . . . is for the teacher to reduce his psychological size (Bolton and Boyer, 1971, p. 5).

Barnes-McConnell says that "Being successful as a discussion leader requires an attitude of openness and mutual enquiry on the part of the instructor to encourage student participation and support the development of a basic level of trust within the group" (Barnes-McConnell, in Milton, 1978, p. 65). She adds that faculty members will be more successful if they view themselves less as judges or dispensers of wisdom and more as resource persons.

Adult students are even more likely than younger students to be resistant toward instruction presented as dogma without opportunity for discussion and rebuttal. Discussion techniques "satisfy the adult's need for active learning and, what is more, are better for overcoming resistance to new ideas than are more dogmatic methods based upon persuasion by an instructor" (Olmstead, 1974, p. 80).

Some university faculty members have traditionally viewed themselves as the sole authority figures in their classrooms and have described their role as teachers as being transmitters of the information they possess to their students. Other faculty members, however, would describe themselves primarily as facilitators of student learning; in this role they would serve as stimulators and as resource persons, but the learning is student-directed and the teacher can only encourage and assist in this process. Of these two philosophies, the latter is clearly more conducive to the utilization of group interaction techniques. For in order to successfully implement such techniques, an instructor needs (again, at least temporarily) to drop her autocratic manner, to desist from her expert/authority role, and to be humble enough to become a co-learner with the students.

How is one to effect the personal transformation necessary to make this consequential shift in roles? One way is to consciously shift attention from what and how the teacher is teaching to what and how students are learning. And how does one find out about that? The easiest way may be the best way: engaging students, individually and in groups, about the what and how of their learning. Some of this can be done in class—intruding into subject matter time to be sure, but still kept within the framework of the learning objectives of the course. Another part can well take place outside where some of the constraints of the classroom are removed and where the common problems of teaching and learning can be faced.

A shift in perspective may come from reflection upon the outcomes, not only for the students but for the teacher as well. If one loses something of one's authority, he or she may gain in a different kind of trust and respect from the students. When I first began teaching about twenty years ago, students respected teachers just because they were teachers. That respect has diminished in the past two decades. The situation as I see it now is that while respect from students can no longer be situationally demanded, it can be earned by being both respectful of them and of one's subject matter. Professors in their specialized subject matters know a great deal more than students; students know a good many things professors do not know. Respecting both kinds of knowing may be at the heart of both the teacher's and student's learning.

Benefits of Interactive Techniques

If more favorable student responses may have to be taken somewhat on trust, contemplating gains in student learning is not purely speculation. Research into interactive processes supports a number of

important outcomes: students become active rather than passive participants in the learning process; students retain the information longer;
various interactive techniques are democratic processes and give students experience in cooperating and collaborating with others; problem-solving and critical thinking skills are best served in discussion
contexts; students can reality-test their ideas within a microcosm of
society; students develop feelings of psychological ownership of or identification with a class; some students learn better in a group situation
than they do individually; self-esteem is enhanced by class participation; students are given the opportunity to clarify their values and
beliefs; student motivation for future learning is increased; student attitudes are more likely to change in a more open classroom environment;
and the instructor is able to receive informal feedback about the progress and attitudes of the students throughout the semester.

In a well-handled small group discussion, it can be assumed
that at least two purposes will be accomplished: "students get new
insights into problems by hearing many different viewpoints and by
having their own ideas critiqued, and . . . they learn new ways of
behaving to which they are committed because of group discussion and
decision" (Olmstead, 1974, p. 92).

With all of its advantages, however, group discussion is not a
panacea. Used properly and knowledgeably to accomplish appropriate
course objectives, it is beneficial and usually enjoyable for both instructor and students. Research continues to indicate that no one strategy is
better than any other with regard to attaining learning objectives, but
used appropriately, each strategy may have its place. Perhaps the
greatest drawback from the instructor's point of view is that group work
is so time-consuming.

In the course of exploring what is to be gained with respect to
student response and student learning, teachers may find themselves
setting aside some of the myths surrounding the utilization of a discus-
sion/interaction technique: that it is only a frill to be added to other
techniques which cannot stand alone as a way for students to achieve
course objectives; that it can only be used with small classes; that it is a
technique suitable only to the social sciences or humanities; and that
any instructor who wants to can do it well with very little preparation.

Contrary to the myth that group discussion is merely a frill is
Barnes-McConnell's well-supported assertion that "the discussion process can be the principal means by which course objectives are attained"
(in Milton, 1978, p. 62). Properly structured, a group technique is not
the sharing of unfounded notions or incorrect information. The myth
that holds that group discussion activities are only possible with small
classes is also inaccurate. Although different strategies are necessary,
small group discussions can be used with classes of almost any size by

dividing the class into smaller subunits. Barnes-McConnell says: "large groups of fifty, seventy-five, one hundred, or more can be broken up into small groups in different parts of the room, facilities permitting. In this case, the instructor can float from group to group to monitor activity. Although the noise level may be a bit high, this can contribute to the excitement up to a certain point rather than being a source of worry" (in Milton, 1978, p. 64). Nor is it true that small group interaction techniques are limited to certain subject matters. They are being used in university classrooms today in almost every field including the sciences, engineering, the arts, and the professional schools. The techniques are amazingly adaptable in that they can be used only once or twice during the semester to teach certain specific areas of content, or they can be the primary daily instructional strategy for a unit or an entire course. Although certain strategies are more commonly found in certain disciplines such as law (the Harvard Case Study) and economics (simulation techniques), there is really no subject matter field that cannot beneficially use some variation of some interactive technique.

Finally, instructors who have tried a small group technique or a group discussion know that preplanning is as essential as it is when one prepares a lecture, and that the instructor's presence during its implementation is just as necessary. Preplanning includes the same areas of concern as do the presentational modes — for example, the formulation of instructional competencies or objectives, time estimations, the specific planning of the implementation of strategy, and evaluation procedures. Interactive techniques, as a matter of fact, are more likely to fail if done in a slipshod manner than are non-interactive techniques. Because more people are involved and the responsibility for accomplishing the goals is more diffused, extra care must be taken to see that the activities are clearly and succinctly structured, and that sufficient time and resources have been allocated to ensure their successful completion.

In general, groups will have one or more of the following purposes: to solve a problem; to complete a task; to reach a conclusion; to consider an issue from a variety of points of view; to more thoroughly understand and apply a concept; to gain additional information; to learn specific techniques and skills; to stimulate new and creative ideas; to aid in analysis and synthesis; to share ideas, experiences, and opinions. Depending upon the purpose to be accomplished, very different techniques would be indicated: "the importance of a method lies not in itself but in how well it accomplishes the purposes of the instructor" (Olmstead, 1974, p. 76).

Many small group interaction techniques have in common the presentation of a stimulus-situation by the instructor to the students to which the students then react in some assigned manner such as arriving at a solution, solving the problem, listing the pros and cons, or simply sharing their individual opinions or experiences. The initial stimulus-situation can be a film, video or audio tape, a book, an article, a legal brief, a case history or study, or a scientific problem. The essence of this technique is that the group discussants must have some common experience with which they all begin. This experience can of course also be current as in the case of a field trip students have taken together, or a research project they have conducted as a group.

The *case study* method, a traditional tool in such graduate fields as law, medicine, and social work, is one of the most frequently used group techniques that employs an initial stimulus. According to the editors of *Change Magazine* in their *Guide to Effective Teaching* (1978):

> The technique involves analysis of statements of problems or issues drawn from life, or simulating life, in the context in which they occurred over a set period of time. The purposes of the case technique are to teach students to select significant from less important factors and to apply principles and theories to the solution of the problem or the resolution of the issue.
>
> Cases can be open ended with the solution not identified or closed with the actual solution indicated or alternate solutions posed . . . Most cases used with undergraduates should be accompanied by a set of questions that help the student analyze the case. Questions should deal specifically with how the problem or issue is defined, how it is analyzed by persons in the case, how it is or would be solved, the degree of objectivity of persons involved, their level of sophistication in approaching the problem or issue, and the possible consequences and impacts of solutions as well as problems (p. 80).

There are many interesting variations of the case study such as the Harvard Method (a carefully disciplined rationale encompassing case preparation, lengthy advance preparation by students, discussion leading and method of analysis); the abbreviated case (a greatly abbreviated case that can even be assigned at the beginning of the class period, individually read, and then discussed by the group); the dramatized case (wherein a short open-ended case is presented on either film or video tape and the group discusses issues and solutions); and the incident-process method. The incident-process method is one of the most exciting methods available if the purpose is to systematically teach students to seek out relevant information. Developed by Pigors and

Pigors (1961), the technique involves the presentation to the students of a brief incident requiring adjudication and decision. The group's task is to decide what additional information is required, but the instructor cannot provide information unless it is specifically requested. At the end of the allocated time for students to question the teacher: "students may finally be required to decide a case on the basis of only partial information because they failed to ferret out everything needed to make a valid decision. After obtaining the desired information, each [student] writes his decision and the supporting reasons for it. The decisions are presented publicly and debated with pleasure by the leader toward arriving at a common conclusion. The students then hear the real decision and analyze the adequacy or inadequacy of their fact finding and decision making in contrast with it"(Olmstead, 1974, p. 101).

Another general category of small-group techniques can be termed *leaderless group discussions*. This includes activities (topic discussions and buzz sessions, for example), for which a formal leader has not been designated and in which the instructor does not participate. In these cases the role of the teacher is to assign the topic, problem, or issue to be discussed, divide the class into small groups, and specify the amount of time to be allocated. Olmstead (1974) notes that "the purpose is to generate more effective learning by overcoming the formalities inherent in large classes through subgrouping and spontaneous discussion" (p. 96). These group discussions may either precede or follow a presentation of content by the instructor, and they may or may not be followed by some kind of reporting by the individual groups. Reporting is particularly useful in letting the students know where their opinions fall with respect to the class norm. In cases, for example, where one student may have taken a minority stand within his or her own small group, the student may learn during the reporting panel discussion (during which time a recorder from each small group reports) that his position was the position taken by the majority of the students in several other small groups.

Finally, there are a variety of techniques which are more generally known because they have been so frequently used in civic organizations and in public schools: *brainstorming* (where group members suggest in rapid-fire order all the possible solutions they can think of and no criticism is initially allowed); *symposium* (a series of short speeches on different aspects of a topic given by the students in front of their classmates); *role playing* (a brief, spontaneous and unrehearsed acting out of a human conflict situation by two or more persons for the purpose of analysis by the class); *panel discussion* (a discussion in conversational form with a leader in front of the class); *debate discussion* (a pro and con discussion of a controversial issue by groups representative of each side); and *committee problem solving* (wherein a specific problem is presented to a group for its group solution or for individual solutions made after the group discussion).

Guidelines

With all that said, how does an instructor actually do group work? What tips and guidelines should direct planning and actual implementation within one's classroom?

Perhaps the single most important thing an instructor can do is to establish clear objectives for the group activity or discussion and to communicate these objectives to the students. These may be distributed to the students in advance as hand-out materials. Gage and Berliner (1975, p. 532) provide an example of such objectives:

> After viewing the film on the origins of science, the students will discuss the improvements science offered over alchemy, and the four major reasons for the popular resistance to scientific methods.
>
> After reading the descriptions on alternative sources of energy, the students will discuss the possibilities of bringing such ideas to fruition, their economic feasibility, the time it would take, the government's role, and the environmental impact of the various energy suppliers. Five forty-five-minute discussions of these issues will be conducted.

After establishing and communicating such objectives, a technique should be selected which best accomplishes that purpose, keeping in mind that most experienced teachers modify the available techniques to suit their own needs.

With university-age students, discussion groups containing six or seven students each are ideal, but this can vary depending upon total class size and the nature of the task to be accomplished. The larger the group, however, the fewer persons can have a chance to be heard, and the more likely some students will be intimidated. Groups containing fewer than four students will not function well either. An examination by Gibb (1951) observed groups ranging in size from one to ninety-six and found that the number of solutions produced for a problem-solving task was a negatively accelerating function of size (Davis, 1969, p. 72). Davis further notes that "changes in personal and interpersonal processes that occur with an increase in group size have primarily negative implications for performance—in spite of positive returns to be expected from an increase in potential resources" (p. 73). McKeachie (1969) says: "Since group members may be less likely to express divergent opinions in large groups than in small groups, we might venture the paradoxical hypothesis that the larger the group, the more effect a few outspoken members are likely to have in determining the success of discussion" (p. 81).

An easy way to break a large group into smaller subgroups is just to have students count off up to the total number of groups you plan to have. Then instruct the "one's" to meet by your desk, the "two's" by the door, and so on. If the students are experienced with group process (and if the weather or facilities permit) sometimes the subgroups may be allowed to find a space for themselves, like adjoining hallways or classrooms or outside on the grass. Be sure to keep track of them, however, as you will need to move from group to group during the process. Beginning groups need close supervision; it is tempting for them to lapse into small talk when there is no instructor to oversee.

The subgroups can of course be formed in much more sophisticated ways such as by using sociometric questionnaires or by teacher assignment based upon a more desirable combination. In a sociometric questionnaire students who know one another well can identify which of their classmates they would enjoy doing a group project with or being in a group discussion with. Groups can then be formed by clustering those students together who have opted to work with one another. This is a very good technique to use when the work groups will be in existence throughout the semester or when an important part of their grade will be determined by the group's product. Teacher-assisted group compositions can only be done after the semester is well under way. The advantages would be that one could more evenly balance the group with regard to motivational level or level of verbal participation, and, depending upon the content being taught, by majority and minority opinions. (These opinions could be ascertained by a brief questionnaire.) The research indicates that one dissenter in a group will more likely concede (even when correct), but two within a group (even if their areas of dissent are different) are less likely to.

Although techniques differ for getting groups started on their activities, a few general guidelines may be helpful. If the group is leaderless (as in buzz groups or topic discussions), the group's general goals, procedures, and timetable should be made very clear to all groups in advance. It is helpful to write this information on the chalkboard or to hand it out in mimeographed form to each class member. Generally it is better to give all verbal instructions before the class is broken into subunits.

If the goal of the group interaction is to solve a problem, the following problem-solving sequence of steps (drawing upon John Dewey in 1933, p. 107-118) will be helpful: (1) an awareness of the problem is developed; (2) the nature of the problem is defined; (3) solutions are suggested to solve the problem; (4) the suggested solutions are compared and evaluated; (5) the best solution is selected; (6) the selected solution is put into effect.

If students serve as small group leaders (and this is usually a very desirable procedure), the class needs to be given instructions before they break into subgroups about the selection of discussion leaders and the responsibilities of the leader and the group. If reporting to the whole group is envisioned, provisions for recording and reporting should be made.

The leader should assume the following responsibilities within the group (these can be written on the chalkboard):

- See that the group members place their chairs in a circle where every member can see and face every other member.
- Be sure everyone in the group understands the assignment or objective and the time allowed for completing it.
- Keep the group on the subject and on time. Remind them occasionally how much time is left. Bring them back to the subject if they stray.
- Encourage quiet members to contribute.
- If everyone tries to talk at once, suggest that each proceed in order around the circle giving everyone some appropriate amount of time to state his/her position. This can be repeated as necessary.
- The leader should not do most of the talking while he or she is serving as leader. The leader's job is to see that the group accomplishes its goal — not to accomplish it for them.
- When the discussion wanders, restate the question and get a new start.
- Summarize (or ask one of the group members to) at the end of the discussion and throughout, if appropriate.

While the small groups are working, it is very important for the instructor to move about the room, stopping briefly at each small group and checking to see if instructions are being followed and if the discussion is moving along well. This group-to-group visiting will provide valuable information about areas of confusion or factual inaccuracy as well as whether or not directions were clear and complete enough.

The first time or two that these group-discussion procedures are used, it would be wise to allow ten to fifteen minutes after the completion of the process to get verbal feedback from the class as to the use of the process itself. This can be an informal give and take, or it can be more structured by asking each group to report on the problems they had (if any) in actually carrying out its tasks. Sometimes very simple factors can cause the technique to be unsuccessful, such as insufficient space where the groups are too close to other groups to concentrate upon what people in their own group are saying. Sometimes the reason is that the group leader did not function well; at other times it is because the instructor's directions or objectives were unclear.

Wallen suggests that if a group is having trouble getting work done it may need to shift from working on the task to discussing the interaction and feelings of the members about what is going on. Symptoms of difficulty he notes include: "excessive hair-splitting or nit-picking; the same points are repeated over and over; suggestions are not even considered; private conversations take place in subgroups; two or three members are doing nearly all of the talking; members take sides and refuse to compromise; ideas are attacked before they are completely expressed; or there is apathetic participation" (Wallen, in Bergquist and Phillips, 1975, p. 149).

A final alternative option to leaderless and student-led groups is the small group discussion led by the instructor. This can be accomplished in the traditional manner only if total class size is twenty or less. For larger classes, however, it may be possible to involve all of the students in the process without actually including all of them in the discussion at the same time. One popular variation is called the "circle-within-a-circle" (or "fish bowl" or "concentric circle"). A small group of students form the inner circle and serve as the initial discussants. The rest of the students form a larger circle around them and listen. After a period of time, persons in the outer circle can move to the inside, or part of them can replace the inner circle if the two groups are not identical in size. Another variation utilizes one empty chair in the circle of discussants. Members of the class who are not in the circle of discussants may enter the discussion group at any point by occupying the chair, expressing their opinion, and then vacating the chair. A final variation is a tap-in procedure whereby class members can tap on a group member's shoulder as a signal that he or she is being replaced. The last two variations allow for a constant interplay of small-group members and class members, but (unlike the "circle-within-a-circle" technique) have the disadvantage that the discussion may become choppy and repetitive. As people move in and out of the group, points tend to be brought up over and over, and it is difficult to arrive at solutions or consensus. For problem-solving discussions these final two variations would not be highly recommended.

In addition to following the suggestions given for students who serve as small group leaders, instructors should also do the following when serving as the group discussion leaders:

1. Explain to the class that your role as group leader or group facilitator (a more descriptive term) will be different from your role as presenter of information. As group leader you will want them to do the talking and to share information

and positions with one another. Suggest that they not address their remarks to you (for they will do this if you do not prevent it), but that they direct their comments to the entire group. If factual inaccuracies should occur, you should of course correct them.

2. When a group member makes a statement that is or could be misinterpreted by other members, clarify it. Ask the member what he means, to give an example, or to elaborate more. Try to restate what he or she said in your own words without adding your own editorial comments.

3. Discourage members who try to monopolize the conversation by avoiding eye contact with them, by asking what others think, or by asking how others react to what has been said.

4. Increase the individual student's sense of participation by encouraging and motivating the group. Enthusiasm, responsiveness, and genuine interest in the subject can be effectively demonstrated without the leader's taking over the group or dominating the discussion.

5. Guard against the discussion's losing its sense of direction or focus. Some confusion is likely to arise in any discussion and should be respected. But the leader should recognize when it gives away to pointless wandering and be able by a pertinent question or a response to another speaker or by initiating a line of inquiry to restore a sense of movement or focus even within a freely-ranging discussion.

6. Summarize, as it may appear necessary, the course of a discussion which has proceeded to a point of useful clarification. Such a summary may be a way of getting a faltering discussion back on track or of shifting from a subtopic that has been sufficiently explored to other aspects of the main topic.

7. Stimulate individual thinking and responding as a means of achieving the group's purpose. Instead of "Do we all agree," say: "Who doesn't agree with that? Will someone try to put into words a counter position?"

8. Encourage students to freely question one another's ideas, but to do so in a friendly manner. This is not an encounter or a sensitivity group; do not allow people to hurt one another or to delve into personal matters. Keep conflict related to ideas or issues, not personalities.

9. Do not be uncomfortable when no one is talking; thinking is important too.

10. Resist being judgmental and avoid dominating the discus-

sion verbally or nonverbally, or becoming .he resident expert-in-the-group. When students try to put you back into the authority role (and they will), throw the question back to the group. If you continue to sense that your role as discussion leader is precluding the students from active (or honest) participation, let a student lead the discussion, and you become the group's external resource person.

Process Evaluation

Most instructors who experiment with a small group technique are curious to receive feedback regarding its effectiveness. There is a plethora of instruments designed to provide this feedback. Rosenfield (1976) suggests a simple nine-point questionnaire that may be answered by individual group participants and by the instructor at the conclusion of the discussion:

1. Am I satisfied with the conclusions reached in the discussion?
2. Am I satisfied with the behavior of the participants? With my own behavior?
3. Did the group follow a logical and orderly approach to the problem, one which was easily understood by all?
4. Did the sequence followed by the group help solve the problem?
5. Am I satisfied with the contributions made by the other group members?
6. Am I satisfied with my contributions?
7. Have I gained new insights, new information, new solutions, or a new understanding of the problem? Am I better for having participated in or having observed the discussion?
8. Was the leadership adequate, or could it have better served the group?
9. What could have been done to make this a better discussion? (p. 88).

The results of this analytical questionnaire can also be used as the content for a wrap-up group discussion.

Perhaps the simplest way to solicit written feedback, however, is to ask each student at the end of the period to briefly state in writing how he or she felt about today's session. Ask for these to be turned in unsigned or signed (student's preference).

Developing an effective interactive teaching style involves more than a mastery of discussion techniques. Yet only by increasing one's skill in encouraging others to take an active part in learning is one likely to be effective. As one's own teaching role may seem to diminish, so may one perceive a growth in students' active engagement in teaching themselves. The satisfaction a teacher often gets from an excellent performance may give way to as great a satisfaction in seeing a greater number of students perform well.

In moving to this teaching style, on should not expect too much too soon. Students who are used to being passive listeners must be led slowly into assuming more active, involved roles during the learning process. In the present university atmosphere, they are likely to find the shifts in expectations made upon them fully as disturbing as the changes in behavior required of the teacher. Discussing the effectiveness of group sessions with the students can provide useful guidance for both teacher and students. It is also a wise idea to ask a colleague or a member of an institution's faculty development office to sit in on group work and to discuss it afterward.

Finally, the fear or reluctance that goes with any shift in behavior may be lessened by finding out about the proposed new directions. Group discussion and small group interaction have been the subject of a substantial amount of formal research as well as of individual trial-and-error which has become part of the anecdotal material on teaching. In any college or university, there are individuals who have developed skills in interaction methods who are willing to share experiences, to be observed, to advise and counsel.

References

Barnes-McConnell, P. W. "Leading Discussions." In O. Milton and Associates (Eds.), *On College Teaching: A Guide to Contemporary Practices.* San Francisco: Jossey-Bass, 1978.

Bolton, C. K., and Boyer, R. K. *One-Way and Two-Way Communication Processes in the Classroom.* Teaching and Learning Monograph Series, vol. 1, no. 1 Cincinnati: Institute for Research and Training in Higher Education, University of Cincinnati, 1971.

Davis, J. H. *Group Performance.* Menlo Park, Calif.: Addison-Wesley, 1969.

Dewey, J. *How We Think.* Boston: Heath, 1933.

Gage, N. L., and Berliner, D. C. "Teaching by the Discussion Method." In N. L. Gage and D. C. Berliner (Eds.), *Educational Psychology.* Chicago: Rand McNally, 1975.

"Guide to Effective Teaching." New York: *Change Magazine,* 1978.

McKeachie, W. J. *Teaching Tips, A Guidebook for the Beginning College Teacher.* (6th ed.) Lexington, Mass.: Heath, 1969.

Olmstead, J. A. *Small-Group Instruction: Theory and Practice.* Alexandria, Va.: Human Resources Research Organization, 1974.

Pigors, P. and Pigors, F. *Case Methodology in Human Relations: The Incident Process.* New York: McGraw-Hill, 1961.

Rosenfield, L. B. *Now That We're All Here . . . Relations in Small Groups.* Columbus, Ohio: Charles E. Merrill, 1976.

Wallen, J. L. "Effective Group Process." In W. H. Bergquist and S. R. Phillips (Eds.), *A Handbook for Faculty Development.* Washington, D.C.: Council for the Advancement of Small Colleges in Association with the College Center of the Finger Lakes, 1975.

Mary Lynn Crow is professor of education and director of the faculty development resource center, University of Texas at Arlington. She was named UTA's Outstanding Teacher in 1972 and a Piper Professor in 1975. Her book, Teaching on Television, *was published by the UTA Center in 1977.*

The authors relate their experience with an instructional development program in which emphasis is placed on assisting faculty to develop desirable teaching behaviors.

Working with Faculty Teaching Behaviors

Bette LaSere Erickson
Glenn R. Erickson

There are a number of ways to think about instruction. Some are conducive to instructional improvement; others are not. For example, though few would claim these days that good teachers are "born, not made," some would argue that teaching is a largely artistic endeavor that defies any attempt at systematic analysis. From this point of view, teaching improvement efforts are either counterproductive in that they may make the "teacher-artist" self-conscious and destroy the performance altogether, or they are futile since little can be done to improve teaching if professors have not been endowed with artistic vision. An alternative view of instruction holds that teaching is amenable to study, that some critical teaching skills and principles can be identified, and that these can be practiced, mastered, and refined by any college professor willing to put his or her mind to the task.

Our work in the Instructional Development Program at the University of Rhode Island is based primarily on the latter view of instruction. As knowledge about teaching and learning emerges from research laboratories and is validated in college classrooms, it becomes increasingly difficult to pretend that we know nothing about effective teaching or to argue that teaching cannot be improved. This is not to say that there is nothing artistic about teaching. On the contrary, outstanding teachers exhibit great artistry in the ways in which they conduct their classes. However, careful analyses of their teaching usually reveal that their artistry rests upon a foundation provided by their mastery of some identifiable teaching skills and their use of some well-established learning principles. We therefore approach our work with the view that teaching does lend itself to rigorous analysis and subsequent improvement.

Taking this view of instruction as a starting point, we have drawn upon educational research and the experiences of college teachers to identify some skills and principles which provide the focus for our work with faculty. While much remains unknown about teaching and there exist many theories about learning, there are some principles to which most modern psychologists subscribe. Psychologists generally agree that students are more likely to accomplish instructional objectives if they are told in understandable terms what those objectives are, if they are provided opportunities to practice the behaviors described in the objectives, if they are given constructive and timely critiques on their practice efforts, if subject matter and instructional activities are made meaningful to them, and if evaluation procedures actually measure the objectives they are intended to measure. While there are many ways to build these principles into instruction, we believe college teachers must find *some* way to incorporate them into their courses.

Similarly, there are some teaching skills which we think college teachers must master if they are to provide effective instruction. Identification of these skills is based on students' descriptions of effective teachers, logical deductions about what a teacher needs to do in order to apply learning principles, and laboratory research into the variables which affect student achievement. Among the skills which are essential for effective teaching are: providing introductions which arouse interest and suggest an organizational framework for instruction; using examples, anecdotes, or illustrations to explain and clarify subject matter; asking questions to stimulate and direct thinking; providing variety in materials and methods; communicating respect and concern for students; constructing valid and reliable examinations; and giving feedback which enables students to monitor their progress.

It is not our intention here to provide an exhaustive list of the principles and skills which characterize effective teaching. We have mentioned some examples in order to illustrate the types of things to which we attend when we analyze teaching and look for ways to improve instruction. We think that by helping professors use these principles and refine these skills, we can help them increase the probabilities that students will accomplish their goals.

Like other instructional improvement programs, ours seeks to provide a variety of services to faculty. We offer colloquia, seminars, workshops, discussion sessions, teaching labs, and individual consultation in a variety of shapes and forms. However, we think the real strength in our program is an individual consultation procedure which we call the Teaching Consultation Process.* Faculty who use this service work with one of us through three major stages of the process: an early-semester analysis of teaching, continuing consultation on improvement strategies, and an end-of-semester analysis of teaching.

In the first of these stages, the early-semester analysis of teaching, we help professors collect relatively comprehensive information about their teaching through interviews, classroom observations, videotape, and a student questionnaire. In the initial interviews, we ask professors to describe their course plans: the subject matter they plan to include, the goals they have defined, the teaching methods they have chosen, and the evaluation procedures they intend to use. The classroom observations and videotape allow us to study how the professor puts these plans into action, and we pay particular attention to the ways they incorporate learning principles and perform teaching skills. The *Teaching Analysis by Students* (TABS) questionnaire asks students to indicate the extent to which they think their instructor needs improvement on some important teaching skills, to provide general ratings of the instructor and the course, and to write comments explaining why they rated the course as they did. The instructor's self-assessment and students' responses to the TABS provide important information which sometimes corroborates our initial impressions and at other times prompts us to take a closer look at the instruction. An important feature of the consultation process is that our early assessment of teaching is based upon information gathered from a variety of sources. Taken together, these perspectives provide a more complete picture of instruction than any single source could provide. We then review all this information with the professor in order to identify teaching strengths, to discover possible areas for improvement, and to define improvement goals.

During the second stage of the consultation process, we try to help instructors find techniques and strategies which will enable them to accomplish their improvement goals. One strategy we employ is to try to help professors capitalize on their teaching strengths. More often than not, professors can solve instructional problems by using skills they already perform effectively in slightly different ways or in somewhat different contexts. For instance, professors who are good at formulating thought-provoking questions can use this strength to improve

---

*The Teaching Consultation Process represents an adaptation of the teaching improvement process originally developed by Michael Melnik, Dwight Allen, and colleagues at the University of Massachusetts' Clinic to Improve University Teaching.

their skills in introducing instructional activities, stimulating interest, providing appropriate practice, or summarizing important information in a class. The identification of teaching strengths is not done just to make professors feel good: knowing what one does well often suggests how one might improve things one does not do so well.

Furthermore, our work during this stage often involves discussing pertinent research, planning and rehearsing classroom activities, practicing particular skills, and evaluating how those activities and skills are working in the classroom. The focus of these discussions, planning sessions, practice exercises, and review meetings differs, depending on the improvement goals defined, but such activities usually enter into our work somewhere along the line.

Finally, our consultation is always tailored to suit the goals and needs of individual professors. To be sure, professors share many of the same instructional problems. However, there is always something unique about the professor's teaching style, about the ways problems manifest themselves, and about the ways possible solutions can be carried out. Furthermore, professors seek different kinds of assistance. Some can take a general suggestion (such as "find techniques to incorporate practice for your objectives") and are able to design instruction accordingly without further consultation. Other professors want to know about the research, see some models, plan class activities in detail, and rehearse those activities before they will try them in their classrooms. In working with faculty during this stage, we not only try to match our suggestions to individual goals and teaching styles, but we also try to adapt our consultation activities to the needs and preferences of the faculty member.

Although consultation on improvement strategies may continue longer than a semester, we usually interrupt our activities before the end of a term in order to conduct an end-of-semester analysis of teaching. Again, we collect information through observations, videotape, and the end-of-semester TABS, which asks students to indicate changes they may have noticed in their instructor's teaching and additional improvements which may be needed. We then review this information with the professor in order to assess progress toward improvement goals and to update our conclusions about teaching strengths and areas for improvement.

In some cases, this final review concludes our work together. Professors discover that they have accomplished their goals, that no new problems have emerged, and that they are satisfied with their teaching. In other cases, the final review reassures professors that they are making progress (or reminds them that problems do not go away if they are ignored) and rekindles their interests in working further. The late-semester review here serves as an intermediate progress check in a consultation relationship which may continue for several semesters.

Although we have tried to identify the key features of the Teaching Consultation Process, it is difficult to describe in general terms something which is first and foremost an individual service. In actual practice, the process works differently for each professor who uses it. Perhaps some examples drawn from our experiences will serve to illustrate these differences.

Some professors discover in the early-semester analysis that they are quite competent teachers. For example, we worked with one professor who explained that he thought he was pretty successful with students, but wanted to check out those feelings. Our analysis confirmed his initial assessment. Students responded favorably on the questionnaire, and their performance on exams suggested that they were accomplishing his objectives. As we observed his class, we were impressed by his skills in using lecture, demonstration, and a variety of small group discussion activities. Although we could think of alternative methods for accomplishing the same goals, there seemed to be no compelling reason why he should use them.

We decided early in our review that the most useful thing we could do was to try to help him recognize what he did that accounted for his success. Thus, we looked closely at the videotape, noting how he incorporated various learning principles and identifying the behaviors which represented effective performance of various skills. Our only suggestion was that he keep up the good work. Since then, he has occasionally stopped by to report that he is experimenting with a new way to provide practice or to make a topic more meaningful or to get students involved in a discussion. He also periodically uses the TABS questionnaire to find out about students' reactions to his teaching. While he claims that our work helped him think more systematically about his teaching, he pursues his teaching improvement goals without much help from us.

Not all professors receive such good news from the early-semester analysis of teaching. At the other extreme is the professor who receives all bad news. We remember walking out of one class thinking that the professor had violated every principle we knew and that his lecture skills represented a caricature of how *not* to conduct a class. Students' responses to the TABS were uniformly negative and their written comments were devastatingly explicit, vivid, and hostile. His self-assessments reflected some dissatisfaction with his teaching, but they made it clear that he was not fully aware of how bad the situation was.

Unfortunately, this is not an unusual profile among professors whom we encounter, and it is not an easy situation to handle. Before we can do anything, we must deal with the shock, discouragement, and anger which sometimes accompanies such negative evaluations. We often feel caught between the need to support and encourage professors so that they view problems as manageable and the need to confront them so that they do not dismiss such information too easily. Then, too, there is the problem of deciding where to begin. It sometimes seems that the most sensible thing would be to stop everything and start from scratch. However, at our university, classes do not stop while teachers redesign courses, nor can professors be relieved of other responsibilities while they pursue intensive programs in pedagogical training. So we approach such situations very pragmatically; that is, we do not claim that we can turn an ineffective teacher into an outstanding one overnight. However, we do believe that we can help professors make some improvements in a semester and that these early accomplishments will provide a foundation for later improvement efforts.

Our first step, then, is to identify a limited focus for improvement efforts — one that will be both manageable and fruitful. In the situation described above, for example, we defined two improvement goals: clarifying objectives for each class session, and providing opportunities for students to practice the behaviors described in the objectives. Throughout the semester, we met twice a week to define the objectives for each class and to design activities for each of those objectives. Our meetings followed a standard pattern. In the first meeting, the instructor reviewed the material he intended to cover, we discussed what students should be able to do with that material, and we translated these expectations into statements of objectives. The instructor then went to prepare the lectures while he assumed responsibility for developing introductions, summaries, and practice exercises. In our second weekly meeting, we put our plans together and worked out the sequences of these instructional events. Gradually, the instructor began assuming more and more responsibility for stating objectives and for planning introductions, summaries, and practice exercises.

We believe we made considerable progress that semester. On the end-of-semester TABS, students said they had seen improvement on several skills related to organization and clarity, and their written comments were more generous and patient in tone, even when they contained recommendations for further improvement. Furthermore, the instructor had prepared a set of course plans which could be used in future semesters. Still, there remained much to be done. The course plans needed revisions before they could be regarded as a coherent and integrated set of instructional activities. And we had ignored many teaching skills which needed attention. However, we had made a beginning. The epilogue to this story is that after four semesters of intensive work, students rated this professor as "one of the most effective (top ten)" or "more effective than most (top 30 percent)."

From time to time, we do encounter professors who represent these extremes. However, a more typical situation is one in which professors discover that they do many things well, but decide their teach-

We have no illusions that the Teaching Consultation Process will solve the myriad problems now facing higher education, or even that it represents the only effective way to work with faculty toward improving their teaching. However, we are convinced that it is an effective service for facilitating instructional improvements—one that allows professors to define their unique teaching styles while developing the skills to use those styles productively.

Reference

Erickson, G. R., and Erickson, B. L. "Improving College Teaching: An Evaluation of a Teaching Consultation Procedure." *Journal of Higher Education,* 1979, *50* (5), 670–673.

Bette LaSere and Glenn R. Erickson direct the Instructional Development Program at the University of Rhode Island. Many of their ideas about working with faculty developed while working in the Clinic to Improve University Teaching at the University of Massachusetts.

Goal setting strategies, training in observation techniques, and microteaching can be used to assist faculty in analyzing their teaching performance and in developing an effective style.

Developing Desirable Teaching Behaviors

Richard E. Ishler
Margaret F. Ishler

The public demand for accountability in education has led to increased research on teacher effectiveness and to the establishment of programs to improve teaching at all levels of education. In colleges and universities, a searching examination of teaching styles and behaviors in relation to teaching effectiveness has barely begun. Efforts to improve college teaching have multiplied in the past decade but such efforts continue to be hampered by the questionable assumption that one need only know a subject thoroughly in order to profess it. Recent research on teacher effectiveness, however, (Borich, 1977; Travers, 1973) makes it clear that there is much more involved in the teaching-learning process than knowledge of the content. Teachers at all levels of the instructional scale must have knowledge of their teaching behaviors and styles and the results these behaviors have on their students if teachers are to grow as effective educators.

This chapter examines an approach to teacher development that increases awareness and builds competence in various teaching behaviors through the activities of diagnosis, goal setting, training in observation techniques, and microteaching. The techniques described have been used successfully with elementary and secondary teachers in teacher development workshops focused on improving selected teaching behaviors. Therefore, these techniques appear to have implications for the improvement of teaching at the college and university level as well.

Before the teacher development program is discussed, the problem of implementing faculty teaching development programs must be acknowledged. At this time in higher education the act of teaching is still a low priority item in the collegiate value system that rewards research, writing, and "grantsmanship" with tenure and advanced academic ranks. Teaching is the expected "given" that is to be performed unexamined and unrewarded (Perlberg, 1977). Centra's (1976) survey of faculty development programs reports an increased level of activities but no clear indication of the effectiveness of current programs and practices. Often, a lack of administrative support makes faculty reluctant to engage in self-confrontation, that stressful experience that does occur when teaching is examined and discrepancies between actual performance and intentions or goals are revealed (Fuller and Manning, 1974). Therefore, if faculty are to engage in a teacher development program, they must feel the need to improve based on some internal or external pressures related to the college reward system. Good teaching as evidenced by objective data collection must become important in tenure and promotion considerations before teaching development programs can gain faculty participation.

The need to examine one's teaching style and behavior must be experienced before growth can take place. This need can arise within the perceptive teacher who senses inadequacies and wants to improve, or the need may be developed through a chairperson who works with new and beginning teachers to improve their skills. The use of student ratings to evaluate teacher effectiveness is a possible way to create needs for teaching development. Assessment by students through student ratings is a practice that is growing rapidly at the college level. Many colleges and universities have introduced policy which requires student evaluation of faculty before they can be promoted (McNeil and Popham, 1973). Such a policy creates the need to examine one's style and teaching behavior as a result of information gained from student ratings, and faculty development thus becomes a vital issue.

In many of the rating forms, designed as questionnaires, students respond on a Likert scale to such items as variety of techniques used, adequacy of student-teacher verbal interaction, adequacy of student input in planning, effectiveness in clarifying the material, and effectiveness of questions asked. The results of these ratings often are distributed to the faculty member and the chairperson to be used for promotion considerations. The teacher is held accountable to the extent that one desires to improve one's ratings, rise in rank, or acquire tenure. The created desire can offset apathy and self-confrontation anxieties and prepare the teacher for the examination of personal teaching style and behaviors.

The examination of teaching behavior can be accomplished best with the aid of a supervisor or department chairperson to assume the leadership role. The chairperson becomes the consultant who works with the teacher through the various stages of teaching development by identifying behaviors to be demonstrated and reinforcing efforts to improve those behaviors (Cooper and Allen, 1971).

Verbal Behaviors

The first step in changing teacher behavior after the need has been established is to build the awareness of one's teaching style and behaviors at the present time in order to have a basis from which to note changes as one works toward newly formed instructional goals. The chairperson or consultant can gather data about the teacher's style and verbal behavior with the use of an instrument such as the Interaction Analysis Category System developed by Ned Flanders (1970), which categorizes the verbal interaction of the classroom through analysis of the verbal behavior of teachers and students. A lesson or lessons can be observed or recorded on video or audio tape for analysis by the teacher and consultant using the IACS. Through the analysis, teachers can identify their teaching styles and verbal behaviors as defined by the Flanders' categories.

Two main styles of teaching are identified with the aid of the IACS: the direct or lecture-centered style, and the indirect or interaction-centered style. The more common style used by teachers in higher education is the direct style, in which the teacher does much of the talking and delivers the content in lecture form or directed activities. The indirect style uses student ideas and questions to stimulate discussion. Thus the IACS gives attention to the amount of freedom and support or direction and control the teacher affords the students. A second group of categories focuses on student talk as to whether it is solicited by the teacher or initiated by the student. A third section examines silence or confusion.

The IACS assumes that the verbal behavior of a teacher is indicative of one's total behavior. An observer, using a statistical procedure, can gather a rather complete picture of how the teacher operates in the class in terms of direct influence (dictating the total class operations—minimizing freedom of the students) or indirect influence (encouraging student initiative—supporting contributions).

The observer records every three seconds the number of the verbal behavior—one through ten—that he hears in the classroom. She can transfer the series of numbers from an observation to a 10 × 10 matrix which enables one to see the patterns and sequence of talk. Categories used to analyze the verbal behavior are: (1) Accepts Feelings, (2) Praises or Encourages, (3) Accepts or Uses Ideas of Student, (4) Asks Questions, (5) Lectures, (6) Gives Directions, (7) Criticizes or Justifies Authority, (8) Student Talk—Response, (9) Student Talk—Initiation, (10) Silence or Confusion. The observer may then see from the matrix, for example, that the teacher spent most of the time asking short questions in the content area and receiving short answers from the students, thus suggesting that questions were on the memory level, not requiring much reasoning. The results from the matrix may be summarized as sequential pairs of statements, total percentages of statements in each category, or the ratio of indirect and direct behaviors explained previously.

There are many advantages to Interaction Analysis, not the least of which is that college or university teachers can use it for self-analysis purposes. This can easily be done by making an audio tape of a class session and then categorizing the interaction using the IACS. As with all the techniques described in this chapter, the key to improving teaching effectiveness rests with the teacher's ability to assess his own teaching. Then, of course, he must set out to systematically improve his teaching based on the data which is collected.

The IACS can be learned by the teacher in a self-development workshop setting in about three hours, enabling the teacher to use the system for self-analysis; to become accurately proficient, however, a minimum of twelve to fifteen hours of work on categorizing is recommended.

The IACS data are not intended to be precise measures of successful or unsuccessful teaching. Interaction Analysis is not to be interpreted qualitatively; rather, it is designed to be an objective indicator of the type of verbal interaction going on in the classroom. Teachers then make the judgment as to whether their actual behavior relates to that which they thought they were exhibiting.

Nonverbal Behaviors

Another aspect of teacher behavior which needs to be diagnosed before and examined during teacher development efforts is one's nonverbal behavior. Nonverbal communication is an important factor in the teacher-learning process. What a teacher says and does is important, but *how* the teacher says what he has to say, *how* he behaves, *how* he expresses his feelings are equally as important. The teacher needs to understand that vocal tones, facial expressions, gestures, actions, and the use of space and time all convey messages to students. When incongruity occurs between the verbal and nonverbal message sent out by the teacher; that is, when a contradiction exists between words and actions, the nonverbal message takes precedence and communicates to the students.

In order for the teacher to become more aware of his nonverbal behavior, an examination of his nonverbal communication can be accomplished through the use of a system (Simon and Boyer, 1974) developed by Charles Galloway (1970). This system, to be used in connection with the IACS, examines the nonverbal behaviors that accompany the verbal behaviors as to whether they are congruent (supportive of the verbal message) or incongruent (contradictory and restrictive to the verbal message).

The following categories are used in the Galloway system:

Flanders Verbal Code	*Galloway Nonverbal Code*
1. Accepts student feeling	Congruent: Supportive behavior Incongruent: Nonsupportive behavior
2. Praises or encourages	Congruent: Reinforcing behavior Incongruent: Neutral or negative behavior
3. Uses student ideas	Implementing: Uses ideas for discussion, questions Perfunctory: Merely repeats
4. Asks questions	Personal: Direct eye contact Impersonal: Lack of direct eye contact
5. Lectures	Responsive: Reacts to feedback Unresponsive: Ignores feedback
6. Gives directions	Involving: Receptive to questions, suggestions Dismissing: Ignores feedback
7. Criticizes or justifies authority	Firm: Directs behavior Harsh: Attacks or expresses anger
8. Student talk (response)	Receptive: Direct eye contact Inattentive: Uninvolved behavior
9. Student talk (initiated)	Receptive: Direct eye contact and directed to point Inattentive: Uninvolved behavior
10. Silence or Confusion	Comforting: Constructive silence Distressing: Disruptive silence or confusion

This system is designed to enable an observer to use the categories, time intervals, and ground rules of the Flanders IACS system while recording the nonverbal dimensions also. By marking a slash to indicate encouraging and congruent behavior, or a dash to indicate restricting and noncongruent behaviors through the coded category number (for example, 2, 3, 4, 8), an observer can record both verbal and nonverbal dimensions of teacher behavior within the three-second behavioral frequency. A circled number is used to enclose the category when teacher behavior is solely nonverbal. This approach appears to be most fruitful when teacher and student behaviors are analyzed from videotapes because the tapes can be viewed several times.

Other nonverbal instruments such as the Love-Roderick Nonverbal Categories and Sample Teacher Behaviors (Chase and Ishler, 1975) can also be used with the Flanders IACS to identify the teacher's nonverbal behaviors. These instruments can be used by the consultant in the initial stage of the development program to diagnose the current state of the teacher's nonverbal skills. The teacher can then be taught to use these nonverbal category systems herself in conjunction with other observation techniques in order to become more aware of her nonverbal behaviors while working with a consultant to upgrade teaching skills.

Technical Skills

The diagnostic phase of teacher development needs to include an examination of the teacher's technical skills as well as the analysis of verbal and nonverbal behaviors before microteaching is brought into the picture for developing competencies. Emphasis on those basic skills breaks down the teaching situation with its myriad of behaviors into specific, basic behaviors that a teacher can identify in his own teaching style and that he can practice to increase competency and confidence.

An initial analysis of the teacher's use of these technical skills can prepare the way for fruitful microteaching sessions in which certain skills identified from the assessment are practiced. The teacher's initial videotape or classroom observation can be analyzed to identify the technical skills being used, the frequency of their use, and the variety of behaviors used in connection with each technical skill.

The technical skills to be examined have been identified by Dwight Allen in his development of the microteaching training techniques (Allen and Ryan, 1969) as being:

- Establishing rapport between students and teachers to obtain immediate involvement in the lesson
- Establishing appropriate frames of reference — being able to teach a lesson from several points of view

- Achieving closure — pulling together major points, tying them in with past knowledge, providing students with a sense of accomplishment
- Using questions effectively — learning different types of questions and the phrasing of them
- Interpreting and reacting to students' classroom behavior
- Learning techniques for encouraging or discouraging classroom interaction
- Providing feedback — how to look for knowledge of results
- Employing rewards and punishments
- Improving ability to analyze and initiate teaching models

When the teacher has completed examining the use of these technical skills in his own teaching style, the teacher needs to identify certain goals based on all the data collected and then move to the next stage — the microteaching experience. The goals should reflect the information learned from the diagnosis stage and the feedback from the student ratings. No developmental program should be undertaken without the diagnosis of the teacher's present style and teaching behaviors (Bergquist and Phillips, 1975).

Practicing Competencies

The practice stage of the teaching development program involves microteaching, a technique widely used in teacher training. This technique can also be an effective method for experienced teachers to use to improve teaching skills (Copeland, 1975; Perlberg, 1976).

Microteaching is based on the assumption that teaching can be reduced to specific skills, which can be examined, demonstrated, practiced, and critiqued with feedback to increase instructional competencies. The skills focused on in microteaching are the nine previously referred to. The teacher concentrates on one technical skill at a time through, first, receiving instruction in the particular skill to be practiced. After the explanation, the teacher sees a brief film or videotape of a teacher demonstrating that skill. The teacher then is requested to teach a short lesson of from five to ten minutes to a small group of students or peers. The lesson may be audiotaped or videotaped and played back for analysis immediately after the presentation. If no tape is available, the teacher analyzes his performance with the aid of the consultant's critique and with written feedback from the students in the group. The teacher then plans an "improved" version of the skill lesson which he reteaches to another group or to that same group (Perlberg, 1976). The teacher keeps receiving training until mastery of that skill can be demonstrated.

As identified by McAleese (1977), microteaching involves four variables that can affect the developmental process: the recording, the consultant, the peer group, and the teacher. The first variable—the recording—can be either audiotape or videotape. Certainly if it is important to the goal of the teacher to provide a visual accounting of the lesson in order to examine the nonverbal behavior, videotape equipment would be necessary. McAleese (1977) points out that the verbal content of the lesson is the most important aspect and, therefore, audio recordings are equally acceptable. However, the authors have used audio recordings with good success and have handled the nonverbal dimension by appointing another member of the group to report on the nonverbal behavior of the teacher. The important point to consider in relation to the recording is not the use of one type of recording over another, but rather the immediacy of the playback. It is important that the teacher have an opportunity to focus on his performance shortly after his presentation. If the teacher can hear and/or see his performance, he will be better able to change the behavior, if necessary. Another point to consider here is that it is not necessary to record the teaching event (Allen and Seifman, 1971). The performance can be analyzed by the whole group and the teacher can receive that feedback before the teaching is repeated.

The second factor—the consultant—is necessary to act as a facilitator, to focus critical remarks on the skill being practiced, and to help with the analysis. It is essential that the consultant be knowledgable about instruction and adept in supervisory skills. It has been the experience of the authors that teachers are more receptive to the microteaching experience if the trainer presents a mini-lesson for critiquing by the group prior to the initial microteaching session. An atmosphere of mutual assistance and support can be fostered through the consultant's willingness to participate in front of the total group and attempt to improve her instructional skills as well.

Using students for subjects in the microlesson is not essential. Peers—the third variable—can serve effectively as the class group and even can add some overtones of positive support for their fellow teacher (McAleese, 1977). Peers can play the role of students and at the same time mentally analyze the presentation. They contribute to the critique, causing it to be a discussion rather than a dialogue between consultant and teacher, and tempering the critical climate of the laboratory situation.

The teacher—the fourth variable—responds to the microteaching situation positively if she is concerned about certain teaching behaviors and their possible effect on the student. The teacher must be motivated to work on these skills. She should have identified, as a result of the initial teaching diagnosis, those teaching behaviors on which she will concentrate. The concern to change in certain areas will motivate the teacher to try to improve.

The mix of faculty within the training group does not seem to upset the receptive climate of the group toward assisting and supporting each other. Faculty with higher rank, such as full professors or administrators, are received as peers if they are participating with mini-lessons as well. Administrators, not having the opportunity to teach classes, may use the mini-lesson technical skills experience to work on conferencing techniques. An appropriate instrument to use to gather objective data about the verbal and nonverbal behavior displayed in the conference situation is the Conference Analysis System (Blumberg, 1974). This tool is modeled on the Flanders IACS system, thus enabling those trained in the IACS to use it easily. Some of the behavior categories are the same skills emphasized in the microteaching technical skills list as well. This category continuity keeps the focus of all the training on the use of effective verbal and nonverbal behaviors.

When using these techniques for developing teaching skills, a group can successfully utilize the following procedure in connection with the microteaching to provide training in analysis and assessment as well as practice in basic teaching skills. The total microteaching group can be made up of as many as nine people or as few as six to fill the several roles. One of the roles is that of peer leader to run the audio or video recorder and conduct the analysis after the mini-lesson. This position is filled by a peer when the consultant is engaged with another group. Another role is that of observer, in which a peer runs the IACS in the mini-lesson in order to obtain practice with the system and to provide feedback to the teacher concerning the verbal behavior displayed and its appropriateness to the skill demonstrated. Another observer role function is to run the Galloway or Love-Roderick Systems to analyze the nonverbal behavior displayed and its appropriateness to emphasize that skill. Another peer can be used to analyze the technical skill itself and all the varied approaches that can be used within that skill to demonstrate it. For example, the skill of establishing rapport can include such behaviors as praising and encouraging students, using humor with the students, using student ideas in discussion, and using a nod, smile, or other such gesture to praise students. The teacher will be provided with a list of such behaviors as they are used. This position, as well as the leader's, can be eliminated if the group is kept at six. The rest of the trainee group serves as the class for the mini-lesson. These people are encouraged to respond to teacher questions in the manner of a student operating at a designated grade or experience level.

The microteaching lesson itself must concentrate on one skill at a time. Although other skills will be used in the lesson, the emphasis must be on the successful integration of one skill with the lesson content. At the conclusion of each analysis following the mini-lesson, the teacher may move to another group to present the lesson again, or he may reteach the lesson to the same group. The members of the group change positions with each new presenter. This movement enables all teacher trainees to participate in a variety of roles during the training period, including observer, analyst, learner, and leader.

An effective evaluation for the participants in such a workshop is their making and submitting to the teacher an audiotaping of a class session in which they have demonstrated the technical skill or skills they are concerned about improving. The tape should be analyzed in a brief report that notes the variety of behaviors used to emphasize instructional skills.

The value of using microteaching in relation with observation training for faculty development in-service programs can be identified as follows:

- The approach increases the awareness of teachers toward their teaching styles and behaviors
- The approach suggests alternative behaviors that can be used to reach instructional goals
- The approach provides opportunity for practicing skills teachers feel they need to concentrate on
- The approach provides teachers an opportunity to learn different teaching styles
- The approach provides immediate knowledge and information about the teacher's performance which can help modify teacher behavior (Meier, 1968).

Summary

Helping teachers to examine and expand their teaching styles and behaviors is a difficult task unless the teacher is motivated through a felt need. This need could come through dissatisfaction with student ratings or from some other external stimulus such as a department in-service workshop.

An effective model to use in this faculty development venture is outlined in the following steps. The teacher shall:

- Submit to a diagnosis of one's teaching style and behaviors using audiotaping and/or videotaping with observation systems to gather objective data
- Formulate several specific objectives concerning teaching behaviors as a result of the diagnostic analysis

- Learn several observation systems that can be used to gather data about one's teaching style and behaviors
- Explain technical skills of teaching with discussion, audiovisuals, and demonstration practice before microteaching lessons
- Practice teaching skills in microteaching sessions so that skills can be analyzed and retaught
- Use observation systems in microteaching sessions to gather objective evidence about behaviors demonstrated in the mini-lesson

This observation and microteaching training technique has been used successfully with in-service work at Bowling Green State University with teachers over the last several years. A less formal system has been used by Kiyo Morimoto (1972) at Harvard University for a decade. His work with teaching fellows has basically consisted of small group critiques of tape-recorded teaching performances. A number of colleges within universities now have video recording and playback facilities enabling faculty to observe their teaching performances privately or with colleagues. Current research does indicate that using a microteaching format can result in changes in teacher behaviors such as increasing the repertoire of teaching behaviors (Copper and Allen, 1971).

As more in-service work in teaching at the college level becomes available, the greater the potential becomes for college teachers to master the instructional process as well as the knowledge of content. With the aid of carefully planned programs such as the one described herein, teaching styles and behaviors can be improved to increase teaching effectiveness.

References

Allen, D. W., and Ryan K. *MicroTeaching.* Reading, Mass.: Addison-Wesley, 1969.

Allen, D. W., and Seifman, E. (Eds.). *The Teacher's Handbook.* Glenview, Ill.: Scott, Foresman, 1971.

Bergquist, W. H., and Phillips, S. R. "Components of an Effective Faculty Development Program," *Journal of Higher Education,* 1975, *46,* 177–212.

Blumberg, A. *Supervisors and Teachers.* Berkeley, Calif.: McCutchan, 1974.

Borich, G. *The Appraisal of Teaching.* Reading, Mass.: Addison-Wesley, 1977.

Centra, J. *Faculty Development Practices in U.S. Colleges and Universities.* Princeton, N.J.: Educational Testing Service, 1976.

Chase, D. J., and Ishler, M. F. *Teaching in a Competency-Based Program.* Dubuque, Iowa: Kendall/Hunt, 1975.

Cooper, J. M., and Allen, D. W. "MicroTeaching: History and Present Status." In *MicroTeaching, Selected Papers.* Washington, D.C.: Association of Teacher Educators, Research Bulletin 9, 1971.

Copeland, W. D. "The Relationship Between MicroTeaching and Student Teacher Classroom Performance." *Journal of Educational Research,* 1975, *68,* 289–293.

Flanders, N. A. *Analyzing Teacher Behavior.* Reading, Mass.: Addison-Wesley, 1970.

Fuller, F. F., and Manning, B. A. "Self-Confrontation Reviewed: A Conceptualization for Video Playback in Teacher Education." *Review of Educational Research,* 1974, *43* (4), 469-528.

Galloway, C. M. *Teaching Is Communicating: Nonverbal Language in the Classroom.* Washington, D.C.: Association for Studying Teaching, Bulletin No. 29, 1970.

McAleese, R. *An Archetype of Self-Confrontation in Teacher Training.* Aberdeen, Scotland: University of Aberdeen, 1977.

McNeil, J. D., and Popham, W. J. "The Assessment of Teacher Competence." In R. M. Travers (Ed.), *Second Handbook of Research in Teaching.* Chicago: Rand McNally, 1973.

Meier, H. "Rationale for and Application of MicroTeaching to Improve Teaching." *Journal of Teacher Education,* 1968, *19,* 145-159.

Morimoto, K. "Supervising Teachers in Groups." In R. Mosher and D. Purpel (Eds.), *Supervision: The Reluctant Profession.* Boston: Houghton Mifflin, 1972.

Perlberg, A. "The Use of Laboratory Systems in Improving University Teaching." *Higher Education,* 1976, *5,* 135-151.

Perlberg, A. "Evaluation of Instruction in Higher Education—Some Critical Issues." Paper presented at the Third International Conference, Improving University Teaching, 1977.

Simon, A., and Boyer, E. *Mirrors for Behavior III.* Wyncote, Pa.: Communication Materials Center, 1974.

Travers, R. W. (Ed.). *Second Handbook of Research on Teaching.* Chicago: Rand McNally, 1973.

Richard E. Ishler is dean of the School of Education and Psychology, Emporia State University, coming there in 1978 from the University of Toledo. His wife, Margaret F. Ishler, who collaborated with him on this chapter, is associate professor of Education at Bowling Green State University.

*Using faculty growth contracts can make the reward system
more responsive to teaching and can assist individual
faculty members in developing their teaching strengths
in specific directions.*

Faculty Growth Contracts

Peter Seldin

Only a handful of colleges and universities have ongoing programs that
encourage faculty self-development. The general advice on most campuses is "publish more," "work on teaching," and "join more committees." Such advice is short on the specifics needed for faculty professional growth.

Drucker (1977, p. 24) underscores the point in the *Chronicle of
Higher Education* that "faculty members need an organized and directed
development effort." This is missing on most American campuses.
Institutions of higher education have yet to offer a concerted administrative push in this direction.

For the most part, the approach to faculty development is to
urge faculty members to attend in-service courses and workshops dealing with the improvement of instructional skills. This is a good but
limited goal. It is also based on the amorphous belief that all faculty
members share the same needs in order to perform acceptably. Yet
there is no magical and fixed set of faculty skills that automatically
guarantees superior teaching. Many professors have developed their
own unique and diverse blends of classroom success.

True, some institutions are developing methodologies to improve
classroom teaching. The feedback approach is an example. It relies on
student ratings, videotapes and classroom observation to help pinpoint
teaching performance in dire need of improvement. Practically, however, many of these programs, laudable in themselves, fail to get pro-

fessors to make needed performance changes. Some programs are not well planned or executed. Some teaching improvement specialists themselves need more training. But the bottom line is that many, if not most, program failures are the direct result of weak incentives for professional change that are, in turn, the direct result of lackluster administrative support. These twin problems—the need for individualizing faculty self-development and for more vigorous administrative support—may be elimininated by the introduction of "faculty growth contracts."

What is a faculty growth contract? It is a plan written by the professor which spells out his self-development, containing his specific goals for the year, each goal accompanied by intended means of accomplishment and assessment, and the required budget.

The introduction of faculty growth contracts offers a systematic approach to defining faculty roles, charting the direction of professional growth, and self-assessing one's performance. Unlike other faculty development approaches, the growth contract anticipates and welcomes change, rather than improvidently changing after the fact. The growth contract is adaptable to an existing faculty development program, or, since it is highly individualized, can constitute the only approach to faculty development in an institution.

Individualizing the program achieves several purposes. First, it helps the professor to reflect on his professional strengths and weaknesses, which can later be translated into feasible goals for the year. As the professor grows, he contributes to the needs of the department and the institution. Second, the program generates evidence by year's end of which goals were achieved and which professional activities fell short.

Historical Rationale

The belt-tightening economics of the 1970s thrust fresh demands on faculty. Along with precipitous drops in funding and student enrollment, faculty accountability became a pressing consideration in colleges and universities. The time was ripe for growth contracts. They enabled institutions to examine individual teaching goals and provided a handy yardstick with which to measure their achievement and thereby size up each member of the faculty.

The concept of the growth contract left intact the genuine need for faculty members, as professionals, to retain the initiative in defining their roles and areas in need of improvement. Thus, growth contracts, while granting faculty members continued freedom to sort out their professional activities, at the same time enhanced the accountability of the faculty members.

The 1950s and 1960s witnessed an era of high faculty mobility and colleges and universities were enriched by fresh ideas, innovative leadership, and new teaching techniques. In turn, the faculty was given continuing incentives for professional improvement and career advancement. This era folded in the 1970s. Today there is an increasing number of faculty competing for a decreasing number of positions. Low faculty turnover makes good job offers scarce.

As a result, colleges and universities are turning to their present faculty for the intellectual vigor supplied in the past by the infusion of new staff from diverse institutions. Somehow the faculty's interest has to be rekindled for classroom experimentation, for rethinking customary teaching techniques, and for reexamining the venerable criteria in decision making and the traditional rewards for accomplishment.

The growth contract fits in nicely with the demands of the times. It keeps faith with academic tradition by allowing each professor to accept primary responsibility for his profesional growth—in the words of Jerry Gaff (1977), "Self development is part of one's professional obligation." And by individualizing each professor's workload and goals, the personal growth contract is easily tied to any institution's reward system.

Current Status

The literature on faculty growth contracts is very recent and strongly supportive. Hodgkinson (1973) calls the growth contract a viable demonstration of professional competency. Seldin (1977) underscores the importance of the department chairman and professor coming to an agreement on performance goals. Buhl and Greenfield (1975) point out that the principles of management by objectives, common to industry, are applicable to performance contracting for faculty. Gross (1976) recognizes the growth contract as effectively encouraging professional development and introducing fair play to the evaluation process. Smith (1976) hails the growth contract as the best approach yet to the blending of faculty development and evaluation in one program. Bare (1979) praises the way the growth contract links department and individual plans without diminishing individual responsibility and self-assessment. Camp (1979, p. 3), a three-year veteran of a Gordon College growth contract, applauds the program for making him a better teacher. His effectiveness "would not have been attained" without the program.

Since the growth contract is a recent arrival on the campus, it has yet to be widely adopted. Even so, in a nationwide survey, Centra (1976) finds almost 40 percent of the responding institutions acknowledging the use of the growth contract. Even more significant than the percentage, however, is the fact that institutions using the growth contract rate it highest in effectiveness of all the faculty development practices.

Today, among the institutions operating a growth contract program, or an adaptation of it, are: Austin College (Texas), New College of the University of Alabama, Gordon College (Massachusetts), Columbus College (Georgia), Ottawa University (Kansas), Medical College of Virginia, and Howard Community College (Maryland).

The growth contracting procedures and policies used by these institutions vary widely, as does the format of the individual contracts in use. On the one hand, one college works up faculty contracts that closely resemble legal compendiums and are accompanied by an explanatory 101-page handbook. On the other hand, another colleague uses free-form contracts born of deep faculty introspection.

Management-by-Objective

Management-by-objective has long been an accepted technique in colleges and universities. A great many institutions employ management-by-objective (MBO) to achieve such worthwhile ends as controlling energy costs by reducing consumption, earning more income from improved billing and collection procedures, increasing investment return in the development office, and bettering performance of maintenance personnel. Now the management-by-objective technique is also being applied to the teaching staff.

The growth contract cycle commences with the department or institution identifying the opportunity, setting the goal, and coming to an agreement on priorities. Each professor's personal and professional goals are then matched with the departmental or institutional goals, with the help of the department chairperson or an advisory committee. The better the match, the more beneficial the goals. When the match is finally negotiated by the professor and the chairperson or committee, the performance goals and the standards with which to measure their achievement are written in specific contractual terms. During the running of the growth contract, feedback and other resource help is provided the professor by the chairperson or committee. The cycle ends when the contract runs out and the professor's achievements and shortcomings are assessed.

The growth contract obviously rests on the assumption that the professor is at least somewhat aware of his personal or professional deficiencies and is genuinely interested in correcting them. The contracts are individualized to fit each professor's perceived needs. The ultimate goal is the development of a strong faculty by complementing diverse teaching strengths. For example, professors specially gifted as facilitators of independent projects should be so assigned; professors who are inspiring lecturers should teach large classes. The best marriage is an exact fit of faculty strengths and department needs.

Theoretically, at least, growth contracts should bring about genuine individualizing of professorial tasks. However, Gordon College, one of the first to introduce faculty growth contracts, reports that a three-year experience with the program has not significantly achieved such individualization. Two possible reasons are offered. One is that small Gordon College (fifty-two professors, about 1,000 students) cannot afford the luxury of selecting assignments by strengths or weaknesses. Secondly, the entire concept of individualization runs counter to the traditional and ingrained academic reward systems that treat all professors alike and brook no professorial weaknesses. The result is the customary deification of the "all-around person" in faculty assignments and in appraisals of their performances (Gordon College, *Professional Development . . . Handbook,* 1979).

As noted, the nationwide demand for accountability has sensitized institutions and external agencies to faculty performance. But faculty members, like most professionals, vigorously resist externally imposed restrictions on their teaching methods. To seek to impose faculty growth contracts on an unprepared and unreceptive faculty is to invite failure. The faculty must "own" the program if it is to succeed. If there is a single virtue in the growth contract it is that its provisions are self-designed and self-imposed. Faculty growth contracts include these specific advantages:

- The professor's development is tailored to his individual faculty workload.
- The department chairperson or advisory committee is drawn into the professor's self-development.
- The collaborative process develops relationships within and across departments and can spur improvements in curriculum design, teaching modes, and research quality.
- The professor's growth plans are tied directly to departmental and institutional needs.
- Each professor gains job satisfaction from planning and achieving his own goals.
- Given the overall faculty responsibilities, there is still room for individual recognition of each professor's strengths and weaknesses.
- Innovation and experimentation are encouraged by minimizing the penalty for failure and maximizing the potential for reward.

- The professor has the opportunity to produce meaningful evidence to support promotion and tenure decisions.
- The professor knows in advance how his performance is going to be evaluated.
- An infusion of fairness and integrity in the evaluative process inevitably strengthens the groundwork for personnel decisions.
- Professors, individually and collectively, tend to perform at a higher level.

Self-Assessment

Since performance goals are a direct outgrowth of self-assessment, the accounting of strengths, weaknesses, likes, and dislikes should be comprehensive, candid, and carefully structured. It should include, for example, the professor's special talent for small group discussions and his interest in further study outside his academic discipline.

The process of self-analysis can be tortuous and unsettling, but the insights of self-understanding can be priceless. The process is more likely to yield fruit if carried out methodically. Bare (1978) recommends that each professor in his or her self-evaluation probe accomplishments and shortcomings in the following areas: (1) contributions to departmental plans or goals, (2) the quality of course content, (3) the effectiveness of the teaching/learning process in certain courses, (4) research, publication, and creative output, (5) advising and counseling students, (6) university service, (7) interaction with colleagues, (8) contribution to professional societies, (9) community service, (10) effectiveness as a clinician or consultant, (11) administrative performance, (12) leadership and interpersonal effectiveness, and (13) evidence of growth and development.

Performance Goals

The form taken by growth contracts varies widely among colleges. East Texas State University, for example, turns out planning documents of integrated individual and departmental plans. Gordon College (Massachusetts) produces formal contracts. New College of the University of Alabama employs an intensive face-to-face discussion with minimal written material. Regardless of the form, the growth contracts must contain a comprehensive self-assessment; specified performance goals resulting from the self-assessment and a timetable for their achievement; a learning and development plan linked to each goal achievement; the means of appraising each achievement; and budgetary or other support needed.

Effectuating growth contracts makes huge demands on the time of the chairperson or advisory comittee. The process involves scrutinizing details about the personal interest and professional life of each professor, as the professor perceives them, and trying to mesh departmental and institutional needs into each professor's plan. Ultimately the growth contracts arrived at individually must be fair collectively.

Easily the most crucial aspect of management-by-objective is the establishment of the professor's goals. They must be specified in writing. The objectives, the criteria, and the appraisal techniques must be specific. So must the scheduling, support and reward, feedback, and development procedure. The colorful, if casual, educational jargon ("behavioral objectives," "change agents") must be banished. Moreover, the performance goals must be significant and meaningful. Their achievement should help the professor grow. And of course these goals must be measurable so that the professor's achievement's and his shortcomings are readily apparent.

To be avoided are performance goals that are too general ("I will make better use of the library"), too trivial ("I will rearrange my books"), or too ambitious ("I will examine the multimedia centers of four institutions in this area each week"). The goals should be realistic and relevant, challenging and significant, attainable and measureable. If the set goal is beyond reach, it will debilitate the professor's enthusiasm. If it is too modest, it will make no contribution to his growth. Buhl and Greenfield (1975) suggest that a good test of a goal is whether the chairperson and professor agree that achieving it is possible, difficult, and relevant to department needs. Should the goals require abandonment in midstream for some reason, they should, however, be redrafted with the same meticulous attention to specifics as given to the original goals.

Advisory Committee

The advisory committee is given a significant role to play in the development of each professor. The initial committee involvement comes after the professor completes his self-assessment and drafts a proposed growth contract. The committee members carefully review the professor's goals, means of achievement, and capacity to be measured. Every procedure must be crystal clear. In the negotiations, the professor's sense of personal freedom to assess himself and draw up a plan for growth must never be in doubt in the professor's mind or in the minds of the committee members. Nonetheless, it may be necessary for the committee members to question and suggest modifications of items in the proposed contract. The committee must not shirk that task. Each of its members is expected to offer the expertise in the area for which each presumably was selected. The tenor of the negotiations must at all times be one of committee assistance to the professor.

At the end of the contract period, the committee should review the professor's estimation of growth and the evidence for it, and provide a written evaluation of accomplishments and growth. For goals not fully realized, the committee may profitably look for the reasons. It may be that the goal was actually too ambitious, or that the professor's interest in the goal languished as his knowledge in the area grew; that the professor managed time poorly; or that the committee faltered in monitoring progress to the goal.

Experience suggests that the advisory committee for optimum effectiveness should consist of three or four persons, including the professor's chairperson. The other committee members can be chosen from colleagues, alumni, or students. Professors from neighboring institutions can also be considered. The major qualification is that those selected be in an advantageous position to help the professor develop and implement his contract. Each committee member's special qualification to serve the professor and to monitor his progress needs spelling out in the contract.

The committee's help in planning and implementing the contract can be the major source of encouragement to the professor to meet his goals. Its members can help clarify the professor's vision of himself, and what he hopes and proposes to accomplish. In the end they can help evaluate his success and fathom the reasons for his failures. Both are necessary for human growth.

One would expect the operation of an advisory committee to create a sense of community on the campus, considering that professors under the benevolent direction of the committee seek discussion and help from each other. In practice, this seems to depend on the institution's purpose in employing growth contracts. On the one hand, at New College of the University of Alabama the growth contract is used exclusively for personal and professional growth. According to academic dean Bernard Sloan, this has resulted in an unusually high degree of collegiality. He attributes this to the separation of the growth contract from the institution's reward system. On the other hand, at Gordon College the faculty members can elect to include their evaluations from their growth contracts for administration consideration in personnel decisions. There is little evidence that this option or the operation of the contract has "significantly broadened our sense of community by bringing together faculty who seldom interact" (Gordon College, *Professional Development . . . Handbook*, 1979, p. 15).

Once the growth contracts are signed, the advisory committee must carefully monitor each professor's progress. This is accomplished by periodic meetings with each professor by the committee or one or two of its members. At the contract's expiration, a final meeting is held to review the goals and to measure their achievement. The professor writes an assessment of his performance, a copy of which goes to each member of the committee. The committee then sends its consensus evalution to the professor. At some institutions the professor may elect to enclose his growth contract, his self-assessment, and the committee's assessment of him in his promotion or tenure portfolio. At other institutions, the growth contract is completely separate from academic personnel decisions.

But in practice, the advisory committee often operates under certain handicaps. First, the staffing of the committee too often tends to be loaded with the professor's friends who are loathe to ruffle him or to cast obstacles in front of his promotion or tenure. Second, the committee at times abdicates its responsibility due to time shortage or some other reasons, and rubber stamps the proposed terms of the professor's growth contract. Third, the committee often tends to be flaccid in its assessment of goal achievement, perhaps as a result of professional reluctance to criticize a colleague.

Today a number of institutions are trying to face these problems by handing the committee members explicit instructions on their responsibilities. Detailed, factual reports are expected on the reasons for each assessment. Accountability is reaching the committee.

Growth Contracts and Rewards

Should the professor's growth contract be directly tied to the institution's reward system? Astin (1974, p. 61) says no. He believes that " any teacher should be able to get advice about teaching, try out new techniques, monitor his or her own performance . . . without prejudice to administrative decisions about tenure." Bernard Sloan agrees. He recognizes the contract as a powerful instrument for faculty development when freed from professorial concern about tenure, promotion, or retention. If applied to personnel decisions, the contract tends to be weakened by political maneuvering and faculty in-fighting.

Bare (1979) also urges the growth contract to be freed from the promotion and tenure process, but for a different reason. At the very heart of the contract is the professor's candid self-appraisal; his improvement depends on his honesty. Such can hardly be the case when the professor, with an eye on promotion, lets the light shine only on his virtues.

Perhaps the best compromise is to allow the professor the option of including in his personnel portfolio the evaluative material from his contract performance. Whether all such material or just portions of it should be included is another matter. Judson Carlberg, an academic dean at Gordon College where professors exercise the option, reports that many professors include the growth contract and the scholarly work in its pursuit, but omit the assessments. Apparently, whatever light shines at the end of the tunnel the professor wants to shine on him.

The length of the growth contract usually conforms to the institution's time limit concerning promotion, tenure, or other personnel decisions. If the professor is eligible for tenure in two years, the contract will be written with that time frame in mind to permit evaluative material on his two-year performance (if the professor agrees) to be examined by the administration.

If anything emerges from the practice of growth contracts, it is that the success of the entire developmental procedure turns on the pure trust placed in it by the professors, the advisory committees, and the administrators. Let one party falter and the system begins to collapse.

Institutional Resources

There is no doubt about the positive value in clarifying the professor's performance goals by the simple act of writing them on paper. It presupposes professorial self-thought. But the professor expects a return commitment in resources from the institution. Graduate assistantships, sabbatical leaves, modest research grants, travel funds, teaching released time, instructional improvement courses, awards, and summer teaching assignments can assist professors. Not every growth contract requires monetary support, but when it does the request should be itemized. If a laboratory manual is to be printed, for example, the exact costs of typing, duplicating, typesetting, printing, and binding should be stated.

It is essential that the administration, in accepting the growth contract, also approve the funding or other resource requests necessary for the contract's implementation. Otherwise, the contract should be returned to the professor for revision.

Climate of Acceptance

If the growth contract is to be warmly embraced by the professor, a climate of acceptance must be created. One way to break ground is to field-test the growth contract on a handful of prestigious professors. The fact that campus leaders are willing to expose in writing their hitherto hidden weaknesses will not be lost on other faculty members. These dry runs give professors and their advisory committees useful experience. Analysis of the purpose and procedure of the contract during the dry runs is inevitable and can produce small but invaluable modifications. This in turn leads to greater acceptance of the contract, in theory and practice, and the anxiety level among the rest of the faculty tends to drop. Given time and personal familiarity with the contract, campus resistance is slowly transformed into acceptance.

Since faculty participation in the contract is voluntary, it might be supposed that the growth program would tend to entice only mediocre professors badly in need of improvement. Not so—most institutions operating faculty growth programs report that their outstanding professors are flocking to the programs.

Case Study

Gordon College now operates a successful individualized faculty development program. No doubt the availability of ample funds since the program's inception in January 1976 has contributed to its success. The program is scheduled to operate for six years with a budget of $350,000. Of this amount $127,000 was granted by the W. K. Kellogg Foundation and the balance was put up by Gordon College. The Kellogg funds are earmarked for only the first four program years. Most of the budgeted money is allocated to growth contracts. In 1978 an average award of $750 went to twenty-eight professors who were not on sabbatical. Typical performance goals in contracts included innovative research, scholarly publication, developing new courses, attending meetings of professional associations, developing new instructional patterns, using consultants, and constructing evaluation techniques.

At Gordon College, the *Professional Development Through Growth Contracts Handbook* (1979) offers instructions to professors participating in the program as presented in the outline that follows:

1. *Preparations of Individual Profile.*
   a. *Self-Assessment.* The professors are asked to write a frank assessment of their strengths, weaknesses, interests, and dislikes. Items are to be directly related to professional responsibilities (for example, an interest in doing more research) and items outside their responsibilities (for example, a need to spend more time with family).
   b. *Statement of Current Roles.* The professors are asked for a comprehensive statement of everything they do, including teaching, scholarly activity, counseling, committee membership, administrative duties, student advising, and coaching athletics. Activity outside the institution (for example, in a professional organization) is to be listed separately.
   c. *Long-Range Projections.* A statement is requested on the

roles and responsibilities the professors would like for themselves two to five years in the future.

d. *Synthesis.* The professors are asked to match their present responsibilities, as stated above, with their strengths, weaknesses, likes, dislikes, and expressed hopes for the future. They are asked to outline the responsibilities they want, year by year, in their two-to-five-year projection. This will form the basis for their annual growth plans. After the initial submission, each professor's Individual Profile is updated periodically if warranted.

2. *First Draft of Annual Individual Development Plan.* Using the broad plans developed in his Individual Profile, each professor designs his own plan for personal and professional growth during the following calendar year. The growth plan must specify performance goals, the means of accomplishing those goals, the means of assessing their accomplishment (extent and quality), and any required budget. There is no limit on the number of goals the professor may attempt to achieve during the year.

3. *Proposed Advisory Committee.* Each professor is required to select an Advisory Committee composed of several persons judged to be specially suitable to assist in the design, implementation and evaluation of the growth plan. Committee members may include colleagues, students, administrators, alumni or individuals at other institutions. The committee number is optional but for each proposed member the expected contribution must be stated.

4. *Summary of Budget Request.* A tabular summary of the budget needed to implement the growth plan must be prepared. In the case of a multiple-year plan, the budget for the first calender year is to be itemized. Expenditures that are not fundable are essentially personal in character; no funding is available as personal remuneration or as pay for student assistants whose principal function is to relieve the professor of his customary responsibilities.

5. *Submission of Profile and First Draft of Annual Plan to the Faculty Development Committee.* Two copies each of the Profile and the First Draft of the professor's growth plan are submitted to the Faculty Development Committee. One committee member is assigned to analyze and prepare a comprehensive, written response containing suggestions for strengthening the plan.

6. *Submission of Final Draft.* Each professor must complete the membership of the Advisory Committee and forward to each member a copy of his Profile, his Annual Development Plan, the written analytical response from the Faculty Development Committee, and a written statement of any changes the professor intends to make in his plan. At a meeting of the professor and his Advisory Committee, pro-

cedures are developed for monitoring his progress. The procedures must be detailed in the Final Draft of the plan (prepared by the professor and the Advisory Committee) and resubmitted for final approval by the Faculty Development Committee.

7. *Implementing the Plan.* After approval and the needed support funds are made available, the professor begins to work toward her performance goals. She periodically meets with members of the Advisory Committee to discuss her progress.

8. *Assessment of Growth.* Toward the end of the calendar year the professor receives two sets of evaluation forms. One set is used by the professor to self-evaluate his performance, and is then forwarded for review by the Advisory Committee. After reviewing the self-evaluation and the supporting evidence, the Committee completes the second set of evaluation forms. Both sets are then returned to the professor who forwards them, with commentary if he wishes, to the Faculty Development Committee. The professor has the option of filing any or all of this material in his official dossier.

It is too early to know whether the growth contract will result in permanent and substantial benefits to institutions of higher education. At Gordon College and elsewhere both the professors and the administration are cautiously optimistic. However, at Passaic County Community College (New Jersey), for example, the program was discontinued after several years of operation because of strained faculty-administration relationships.

One thing is clear. It is highly unlikely that a faculty growth program successful in one institution can be lifted intact by another. Success must be wooed by tailoring the program to the realities of the campus interested in trying it. On each campus the faculty behaviors and teaching styles are inevitably shaped by such factors as resource availability, faculty needs, campus leadership, institutional traditions, community constraints, and campus politics.

The Gordon College *Professional Development Handbook* (1979) contains several pertinent questions to be answered by any college or university interested in introducing the growth contract. Are the feelings of mutual trust on the campus hardy enough and the desire for personal and professional growth earnest enough for professors to be willing to expose publicly their frailties? How really practical is the individualizing of faculty members' roles based on their strengths and weaknesses? Can the campus accommodate to this process? Even when the professor opts for it, is the connection between the growth contract and his promotion or tenure a workable link? Or does it tend to pull the program apart?

With workable answers to these questions and a little bit of luck, the growth contract holds formidable promise to raise individual and collective performance levels.

References

Astin, A. W., and others. *Faculty Development in a Time of Retrenchment.* New Rochelle, N.Y.: *Change Magazine,* 1974.

Bare, A. C. "Contracting Effectively for Individual Growth." In B. T. Massey (Ed.), *Proceedings of the Fifth International Conference on Improving University Teaching.* London: University of Maryland, 1979.

Bare, A. C. "Individual Development Planning in Academic Settings." *Faculty Development and Evaluation in Higher Education,* 1978, *4* (3), 1-9.

Buhl, L., and Greenfield, A. "Contracting for Professional Development in Academe." *Educational Record,* 1975, *56* (2), 111-121.

Camp, R. "A Personal Look." *Planning for Growth.* Wenham, Mass.: Gordon College, 1979.

Centra, J. A. *Faculty Development Practices in U.S. Colleges and Universities.* Princeton, N.J.: Educational Testing Service, 1976.

Drucker, P. F. "The Professor as Featherbedder." *The Chronicle of Higher Education,* January 31, 1977, p. 24.

Gaff, J. G. Personal correspondence, 1977.

Gordon College. *Professional Development Through Growth Contracts Handbook.* Wenham, Mass.: Gordon College, 1979.

Gross, R. F. "Faculty Growth Contracts." *Faculty Development and Evaluation in Higher Education,* 1976, *2* (1), 9-14.

Seldin, P. "Faculty Growth Contracts." Published as an Occasional Paper. London: University of London, 1977.

Smith, A. B. "Faculty Development and Evaluation in Higher Education." *Higher Education Research Report,* No. 8, Washington, D.C.: ERIC, 1976.

Peter Seldin is professor of management at Pace University, Pleasantville, New York. Formerly at Fordham University, he was visiting associate, Institute of Higher Education, University of London in 1976. He has written two books, How Colleges Evaluate Professors *(1975) and* Teaching Professors to Teach *(1977) and is currently completing a third. Peter Seldin has produced about twenty-five articles on faculty development and evaluation in such publications as* The New York Times *and* Change Magazine.

This chapter reflects on further implications of giving attention to teaching styles and faculty behaviors.

Future Considerations and Additional Resources

Kenneth E. Eble

These chapters cover only a part of the territory of teaching style and faculty behavior. Though they make no pretense to inclusiveness, they do indicate current and past interests within the profession as well as some neglects.

Developing a teaching style has never been a foremost concern of college and university professors. The graduate schools put no emphasis upon it, and only teaching itself and the interest it arouses day by day leads some faculty members to consider style and its implications for their effectiveness. In only one sense is this as it should be. And that is that the development of style, as various essays here point out, is more than the acquiring of techniques, the learning of skills, or the conscious deploying of one's resources. Style is what one is; the acquisition of an effective teaching style would probably be the worse if it were made the subject of course work in a graduate curriculum.

But having said that, I think the inattention to teaching style, particularly in the graduate school, is still a major cause of the middling state teaching occupies. If style itself is beyond the reach of graduate school training, attention to teaching is not. Within that majority of disciplines in which college and university teaching is the likely career of those who receive advanced degrees, such attention should be an integral part of degree programs.

The chapters by Joseph Axelrod and John Granrose give personal testimony to this need. They also chart a common experience of graduate students becoming college professors. Granrose's experience with too many mediocre undergraduate teachers developed in him no inclination for teaching as a career. Both he and Axelrod's fictional teacher, Stephen Abbot, had their interest awakened in their graduate work more because of an interest in subject matter than because of examples their professors set. Neither received much formal guidance or assistance in developing teaching skills, much less in considering the importance of working toward an effective teaching style. The introspection that Abbot had forced upon him through his career seems to have been always attended by a feeling that his major interests should be elsewhere. If he seems, to himself and to the reader, to be a mere teaching organism adapting his behavior to changing exterior conditions, it may be because his early education gave him no notion that the ways of teaching and learning might be just as vital concerns, just as much objects of study and thought and examined practice, as the ways of literary form and creation. Both Granrose and Abbot learned somehow, along the way, probably because the living presence of students and the interactions with their own living presences as teachers forced the attention which is the absolute antecedent of learning.

Given the large amount of teaching that graduate assistants do in large universities, there is little excuse in graduate work for not including more wise and effective attention to acquiring teaching skills. The attention given to faculty members experiencing difficulties in teaching — as described by a number of chapters in this volume — has to work against often strongly established habits. How much better it might have been to have had such attention a part of the apprentice teaching experience. All of the techniques now employed in working with established faculty — from the Ericksons' clinical approach to the Ishlers' description of observation techniques — could be employed with a greater promise of success in the graduate schools.

But beyond the acquiring of techniques and the beneficial effects of experimenting with, discussing, and developing teaching skills is the inclining of faculty behaviors toward "inspired teaching," as John Granrose calls it. The modeling that takes place in the graduate schools needs greater numbers of superb teachers to serve as models. And such superb teachers must be enlisted in making the greater mysteries worthy of study even amidst doubts that they can ever be made perfectly clear.

The consistent strain in this collection is one that respects both the greater mysteries of inspired teaching and the lesser mysteries of teaching that proceeds competently along. While none of the authors asserts that all can be known and therefore taught about effective teaching, none backs away from the belief that many useful things about teaching can be taught. Here the basic question is a basic one to all those who take teaching and learning seriously. For when we say "Teaching can be taught," we are defining "taught" in a very broad way. Ultimately, that definition shifts to "learned," and the phrase then becomes "Specific acts, behaviors if you will, of teaching can be learned." Even those terms may be too confining. Instead of "learned," we may wish to say "acquired" or "developed." But the point is that whether we are talking about the teaching of teaching or the teaching of tennis, we must always be mindful of the prime necessity of learning taking place within the person being taught. The ways in which learning takes place are as difficult to describe as any aspect of this complex subject. We do know that in time, with some persons, learning becomes the powerful backhand that seems to know exactly how to respond to the precise characteristics of a ball arriving at such an angle and such a speed and with just such a spin. So it is with a teacher confronting a question from just such a pupil delivered with what precise measure of aggression at just this moment in these particular conditions. The one kind of developing of skills—teaching—surely deserves as much attention as the other—tennis. Both can be learned on the playground, so to speak, with little formal instruction, but neither can be learned well without conscious attention and unremitting practice. Both can be assisted by the professionals who can translate their own seemingly unconscious perfections into conscious behaviors.

If I dwell on these seemingly simple considerations, it is because the profession's willingness to give teaching this kind of purposeful attention is basic to developing effective teachers possessing effective teaching styles. And as I stated at the outset of this collection, dispelling notions that place "style" in an adverse light is a first step. Style is a paradoxical concept applied to teaching as to any other behavior. The truly impressive style, like grace, is or appears to be a natural possession. If it betrays a self-consciousness in the possessor, it moves quickly to affectation. If it seems studied in its bearing, it moves toward techniques wanting in spirit. And yet, an impressive style in any professional calling is among its practitioners' highest attainments. What the profession of teaching might aspire to is dignifying and respecting the acquiring of style which avoids either affectation or pedantry, which does not even call attention to itself but which, being natural, arouses an equally natural and favorable response. As individuals differ and their styles are signs of their difference, so teaching styles would differ. And as young men and women are inclined toward teaching, they would see the acquiring of style as a professional attainment of a high order, at least as important as mastery of a specialized area of knowledge within a discipline. Like that mastery, too, acquiring of a style would be a process, not a completion. Still, like the confidence one gains through patient and prolonged study, so a set of characteristic stances and responses, movements and conjunctions of mind and body and feeling, would arise to provide the indispensable center from which teaching would proceed along the way to a full maturing of style.

It is somewhat easier to talk about faculty behaviors than to talk about teaching style. Behavioral psychology has a long history, and its application to teaching and learning are much a part of contemporary theory and practice. Compared with the attention given it in public school education, however, the attention in higher education is very small. A partial reason is a long-maintained and unfortunate separation between lower and higher education and various degrees of hostility and distrust between colleges of education and other colleges in a modern university. The essays by professors of education and psychology in these pages suggest, at least, that we can speak the same language. What they say about ways of working with groups, of wisely observing teaching, and of learning from those observations is applicable to teaching in any discipline. It further bespeaks the catholicity of teaching and learning to point out that the essayist most strenuously engaged in examining and modifying a teaching style is not a professor of education but of biochemistry and genetics.

Finally, teaching behaviors are obviously influenced by outside forces. The nature of colleges and universities, the patterns of instruction, the regulations covering programs and degrees, and the structure which defines faculty rewards all influence the way college professors go about their work. Peter Seldin's closing chapter faces this array of exterior forces within a specific and important context. The objectives that professors set for themselves are more likely to be achieved when such objectives are recognized and accepted by the institution. Institutional aims are more likely to be fulfilled when they are in harmony with the aims of the individuals who make up an institution. Thus, bringing together individual and institutional aims seems to be a promising direction for the enhancement of teaching. Administrators, particularly deans and department chairpersons, can, by their wise involvement in faculty growth contracts, become a source of great strength in faculty development efforts. In working with growth contracts, faculty members can become supportive colleagues in recognizing the diversity that characterizes teaching responsibilities, strengths, and styles.

Evaluating teaching and faculty development are two major movements of the past decade. Both came into prominence because of the forces described by Joseph Axelrod which promoted many of the reforms of the sixties. And as his Professor Abbot looks pessimistically toward the future, so may observers of these two movements be pessimistic about the lasting and favorable impact of evaluation and faculty development. The changing characteristics of students that bother Professor Abbot have had a serious effect on maintaining responsible student evaluations. The faculty development movememt may have peaked even before it has reached a very high level of effectiveness. But whatever the fate of these current manifestations of attention to teaching, the need remains to develop and maintain teachers who excite and inspire and make a difference to those they meet.

Additional Resources

Faculty behavior covers such a wide territory as to make it difficult to provide a comprehensive bibliography. The specific subjects of style and personality in teaching, however, have not created a large body of resource material. Authors of individual essays have supplied a short number of resources they have found useful in their own teaching and work. The result is a varied list of books, articles, and agencies from which information can be sought.

Association of Teacher Education. *Microteaching: Selected Papers.* Research Bulletin No. 9. Washington, D.C.: Association of Teacher Educators and ERIC Clearinghouse on Teacher Education, 1971.

This monograph is concerned with the history and present status of microteaching, and the function of microteaching in teacher educator programs such as those in Stanford, Brigham Young, and San Jose State College.

Bergquist, W. H., and Phillips, S. R. *A Handbook for Faculty Development.* Vols. 1 and 2. Washington, D.C.: The Council for the Advancement of Small Colleges, 1975, 1977.

These handbooks are uneven but especially useful resources for anyone working with faculty to improve teaching. They include theoretical and reflective essays along with a wide variety of practical exercises and materials for working with faculty and administrators. Volume 1 includes a step-by-step description of the consultation procedure discussed by the Ericksons in Chapter 3.

Bolton, C. K., and Boyer, R. K. "One-Way and Two-Way Communication Processes in the Classroom." *Teaching-Learning Monograph Series,* September 20, 1971, *1* (1).

Containing eleven pages of information comparing one- and two-way communication patterns in the classroom, the *Teaching-Learning Monograph Series* is a publication of the Institute for Research and Training in Higher Education, University of Cincinnati, Cincinnati, Ohio 45221.

Borich, G. *The Appraisal of Teaching.* Reading, Mass.: Addison-Wesley, 1977.
This book examines the conceptional framework and concepts of teaching and includes five chapters of selected readings on different appraisal topics such as "Defining Teacher Competencies," "Measuring Teacher Performance," and "Appraisal Procedures and Techniques."

Buhl, L., and Greenfield, A. "Contracting for Professional Development in Academe." *Educational Record,* 1975, *56* (2), 111–121.
This article advocates that faculty members and chairpersons make contracts containing provisions for professional and personal growth. It presents both theoretical underpinnings and practical pitfalls.

Cartwright, D., and Zander, A. *Group Dynamics, Research and Theory.* (3rd ed.) New York: Harper & Row, 1968.
This is a thorough treatment of the research regarding people in groups and the factors that cause them to behave the way they do.

Clinic to Improve University Teaching. *Working Definitions of Some Technical Skills of Teaching.* Amherst, Mass.: Clinic to Improve University Teaching, University of Massachusetts, undated mimeo. (Available through the ERIC Document Reproduction Service, No. ED 150 910.)
This is an uneven but interesting attempt to explicate some important teaching skills and suggest ways in which faculty could perform them more effectively.

Davis, R. H., Alexander, L. T., and others. *Guides for the Improvement of Instruction in Higher Education.* Nos. 1–13. East Lansing: Instructional Media Center, Michigan State University, 1977.
The Guides provide practical tips to college teachers on how to manage everything from writing useful objectives to evaluating their own instruction. The pamphlets on lecturing (No. 5) and discussion (No. 6) are especially useful.

Educational Horizons: Faculty Development in Higher and Professional Education, Winter 1976–1977, *55.*
A special issue of the journal of Phi Lambda Theta, a professional organization in education devoted to faculty development. Both discipline and institutional models are presented.

Frankena, W. K. (Ed.). *Philosophy of Education.* New York: Macmillan, 1965.

After his clarifying introductory essay, Frankena presents stimulating excerpts from the writings of Dewey, Whitehead, Maritain, and R. S. Peters.

Gordon College. *Professional Development Through Growth Contracts.* Wenham, Mass.: Gordon College, 1979.

This handbook presents general insights and research data on faculty growth contracts. It contains a detailed users manual with step-by-step instructions for developing contracts.

Hennings, D. G. *Mastering Classroom Communication.* Pacific Palisades, Calif.: Goodyear, 1975.

Teaching is viewed as communication in this book that draws together findings of contemporary research on teaching to clarify the teacher's role in classroom communications. The communication process, nonverbal behavior, and verbal behavior are explored in such a way that the teacher can study samples of one's own teaching to become more aware of teaching styles and their effects on communication with students.

Hodgkinson, H. L. "Faculty Reward and Assessment Systems." In B. L. Smith (Ed.), *Tenure Debate.* San Francisco: Jossey-Bass, 1973.

This book establishes a conceptual framework for faculty growth contracts and argues that any legitimate system of faculty assessment should measure faculty competence both in terms of faculty performance and professional growth patterns.

How to Succeed as a New Teacher: A Handbook for Teaching Assistants. New Rochelle, N.Y.: *Change* Magazine Press, 1978.

This sixty-three page booklet adapts the most helpful general material from Stanford University's *Handbook for Teaching Assistants* and UCLA's *What Every TA Should Know.*

Kemp, J. E., and McBeath, R. J. *Lecturing,* (videotape, 55 minutes, black and white). San Jose, Calif.: Faculty and Instructional Development Office, San Jose State University, 1979.

Paperback text and workbook accompany this videotaped series of San Jose professors discussing and demonstrating their style as lecturers.

Kozma, R. B., Belle, L. W., and Williams, G. W. *Instructional Techniques in Higher Education.* Englewood Cliffs, N.J.: Educational Technology Publications, 1978.

The introductory section on the context of college teaching adds a great deal to the subsequent description of some fifteen different teaching techniques. The authors do a nice job of listing the advantages and disadvantages and the most appropriate uses of each technique.

Lucas, F. L. *Style*. New York: Collier Books, 1962.
    Lectures originally given at Cambridge, these essays focus on style in writing, but range much wider in their observations. Professors troubled about emphasizing style in teaching might begin here.

McKeachie, W. J. *Teaching Tips: A Guidebook for the Beginning College Teacher*. (7th ed.) Lexington, Mass.: D. C. Heath, 1978.
    Veteran, as well as beginning, faculty find this an engaging and useful guide in addressing a wide array of issues and problems in college teaching. Each chapter includes practical tips and readable discussions of relevant theory and research.

Medley, D. *Teacher Competence and Teacher Effectiveness: A Review of Process-Product Research*. Washington, D.C.: AACTE, 1977.
    This publication brings together reseach findings on teaching effectiveness along with the interpretive comments of a noted researcher in the education field.

Menges, R. *College Classroom Vignettes*. Evanston, Ill.: The Center for Teaching Professions, Northwestern University, 1978.
    These are videotapes of unstaged classroom performances, each package comprising a tape of about thirty minutes, a printed transcript, leader's guide and other written materials. Sample tape available on request; individual tapes on such subjects as "Teaching Styles," "Attentiveness During Lectures: Nonverbal Cues," and "Helping Students Clarify Ideas," may be purchased.

Milton, O., and Associates. *On College Teaching: A Guide to Contemporary Practices*. San Francisco: Jossey-Bass, 1978.
    A book of readings, each devoted to a different teaching strategy, written by individuals accomplished in those particular styles.

Olmstead, J. A. *Small-Group Instruction: Theory and Practice*. Alexandria, Va.: Human Resources Research Organization, 1974.
    This small paperback describes in detail various methods of small-group instruction including objectives, recommended uses, student and instructor requirements, and time, materials and facilities involved.

Shaw, M. E. *Group Dynamics, The Psychology of Small-Group Behavior*. New York: McGraw-Hill, 1971.

This book provides an integrated treatment of small-group phenomena. Each chapter is concluded by a list of plausible hypotheses which are the most reasonable interpretations that can be made of the phenomena discussed in the chapter.

Sheffield, E. F. *Teaching in the Universities: No One Way.* Montreal: McGill-Queens University Press, 1974.

These personal essays describing how a distinguished group of Canadian university professors go about their work comprise an excellent compendium of teaching styles. Sheffield's essay on how teachers were identified and teaching characteristics that appear to be effective is also excellent.

Sherman, B. R., and Blackburn, R. T. "Personal Characteristics and Teaching Effectiveness of College Faculty." *Journal of Educational Psychology,* 1975, *66,* 124–131.

The importance of personality factors in improving teaching effectiveness based on conclusions of a study conducted at liberal arts colleges is stressed in this article.

Smith, W. B. "Faculty Development and Evaluation in Higher Education." *Higher Education Research Report,* No. 8. Washington, D. C.: ERIC, 1976.

This article describes four distinct faculty development programs and reviews current research findings. The author believes that faculty development and evaluation should be merged and that faculty growth contracts are the best approach to date.

Strunk, W., and White, E. B. *The Elements of Style.* (3rd ed.) New York: Macmillan, 1979.

Although the suggestions in this classic book are directed toward style in writing, many of them, especially in Chapter 5, "An Approach to Style," would also apply to style in teaching.

Weil, M., and Joyce, B. *Information Processing Models of Teaching, Personal Model of Teaching,* and *Social Models of Teaching.* Englewood Cliffs, N. J.: Prentice Hall, 1978.

Each book looks at certain teaching strategies that can be used to accomplish objectives for teachers; for example, the *Social Models* strategies are aimed at facilitating democratic processes and creating a more humane society. Each strategy is presented with its theoretical base, examples of the teaching behavior, suggestions for teacher practice, and methods of evaluation.

Wilson, R. C., and others. *College Professors and Their Impact on Students.* New York: Wiley, 1975.

A careful and broad-based attempt to relate the assessment of characteristics of effective teachers to the learning of students. Chapters 3 and 10 raise important questions related to a teacher's style. own teaching.

Index

New Directions Quarterly Sourcebooks

New Directions for Teaching and Learning is one of several distinct series of quarterly sourcebooks published by Jossey-Bass. The sourcebooks in each series are designed to serve both as *convenient compendiums* of the latest knowledge and practical experience on their topics and as *long-life reference tools*.

One-year, four-sourcebook subscriptions for each series cost $18 for individuals (when paid by personal check) and $30 for institutions, libraries, and agencies. Single copies of earlier sourcebooks are available at $6.95 each *prepaid* (or $7.95 each when *billed*).

A complete listing is given below of the titles and editors-in-chief of the other *New Directions* series. To subscribe, or to receive further information, write: New Directions Subscriptions, Jossey-Bass Inc., Publishers, 433 California Street, San Francisco, California 94104.

New Directions for Child Development
William Damon, Editor-in-Chief

New Directions for Community Colleges
Arthur M. Cohen, Editor-in-Chief
Florence B. Brawer, Associate Editor

New Directions for Continuing Education
Alan B. Knox, Editor-in-Chief

New Directions for Exceptional Children
James J. Gallagher, Editor-in-Chief

New Directions for Experiential Learning
Morris T. Keeton and Pamela J. Tate, Editors-in-Chief

New Directions for Higher Education
JB Lon Hefferlin, Editor-in-Chief

New Directions for Institutional Advancement
A. Westley Rowland, Editor-in-Chief

New Directions for Institutional Research
Marvin W. Peterson, Editor-in-Chief